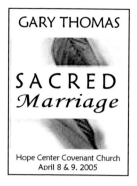

GARY THOMAS

SACRED
Marriage

Hope Center Covenant Church
April 8 & 9, 2005

Randy
Dodd

DEVOTIONS
For A
SACRED
Marriage

Books by Gary Thomas

Authentic Faith
Devotions for a Sacred Marriage
Devotions for Sacred Parenting
The Glorious Pursuit
Not the End but the Road
Sacred Marriage
Sacred Parenting
Sacred Pathways
Seeking the Face of God

To Diane –

GARY L. THOMAS

DEVOTIONS

For A

SACRED

Marriage

The peace of Christ,

Gary Thomas

A Year of
Weekly Devotions
for Couples

ZONDERVAN™

GRAND RAPIDS, MICHIGAN 49530 USA

ZONDERVAN™

Devotions for a Sacred Marriage
Copyright © 2005 by Gary L. Thomas

Requests for information should be addressed to:
Zondervan, *Grand Rapids, Michigan 49530*

Library of Congress Cataloging-in-Publication Data

Thomas, Gary (Gary Lee)
    Devotions for a sacred marriage : a year of weekly devotions for couples /
Gary L. Thomas.
      p. cm.
    Includes bibliographical references (p.   ).
    ISBN-10: 0-310-25595-3 (hardcover)
    ISBN-13: 978-0-310-25595-6
    1. Married people—Prayer-books and devotions—English   I. Title.
BV4596.M3T45 2005
242'.644—dc22
                                                  2004026272

This edition printed on acid-free paper.

Interior design by Michelle Espinoza

Printed in the United States of America

05 06 07 08 09 10 11 /❖ DCI/ 10 9 8 7 6 5 4 3 2 1

To Rob and Jill Takemura, friends for life

Contents

Introduction

While this devotional book consists of 100 percent new material, I based it on the principles first stated in my book *Sacred Marriage*. Although it's not necessary to have read *Sacred Marriage* to enjoy or profit from this book, I would recommend going through *Sacred Marriage* first, and then reading this devotional book with your spouse or small group.

I designed *Devotions for a Sacred Marriage* to be read in fifty-two separate sittings, one a week for a year. Because of the significant challenges it highlights, reading one devotion a day could get a bit tiring. I believe you'll profit more from spending one day a week focusing on your marriage, and six days doing general devotions.

Some have asked, "Why this format?" It originated in part because so many couples requested a follow-up book to *Sacred Marriage* — but that presented a problem. As I've stated many times, *Sacred Marriage* is not a how-to manual. I am neither qualified nor inclined to produce such a book. So what was there to follow up?

That's when a couple graciously providing me a ride to the airport suggested I write a devotional book that would explore some of the *Sacred Marriage* principles from a fresh perspective. I thank them anonymously for leading me in this direction. The writing alone has been a powerful experience for me, as I've been challenged, inspired, and convicted, while grappling with a truth greater than us all.

In fact, I pray that taking this yearlong journey with your spouse will benefit you at least half as much as crafting it did me! If you are married, God has called you into a delightful yet difficult, a problematic yet profound, relationship — but through it all, I have found (and I'm sure you have, too) that marriage is more than worth the pain.

1

The God-Centered Spouse

Let us purify ourselves from everything that contaminates body and spirit, perfecting holiness out of reverence for God.

2 Corinthians 7:1

Greg Nettle, pastor of the RiverTree Christian Church in Massillon, Ohio, was walking to his car after a golf tournament when he realized the remote trunk opener wasn't working. Neither were the automatic door locks. When he finally got inside the car, he saw the fuel gauge reading empty, even though he had filled up on gas less than twenty-four hours before. More frustrating yet, the car would turn over but then immediately die.

After a tow truck delivered the disabled vehicle to the dealership, a mechanic came out to Greg and told him the problem: a bad BCM.

"What's a BCM?"

"The basic control module. It's essentially the car's brain, and once it goes bad, everything starts malfunctioning."

Greg could have insisted on "fixing" the trunk, the door locks, the gas gauge, and any number of problems — but those were merely the symptoms of an overall malfunction.

How often do we do the same thing with marriage! We focus on the symptoms:

- "We need to improve our communication."
- "We need to get better at handling conflict."
- "We need to show more appreciation for each other."
- "We need to have a more unified plan with the children."
- "We need to work harder at keeping the romance alive in our relationship."

We can spend a lifetime focusing on the symptoms, or we can replace the BCM — the basic control module. I believe the BCM for marriage is our *spiritual motivation*.

It all comes down to this: Are you a God-centered spouse or a spouse-centered spouse? A spouse-centered spouse acts nicely toward her husband when he acts nicely toward her. She is accommodating, as long as her husband pays her attention. A spouse-centered husband will go out of his way for his wife, as long as she remains agreeable and affectionate. He'll romance her, as long as he feels rewarded for doing so.

But Paul tells us we are to perfect holiness *out of reverence for God*. Since God is always worthy to be revered, we are always called to holiness; we are always called to love. A God-centered spouse feels more motivated by his or her commitment to God than by whatever response a spouse may give.

Spouse-centered Christians try to make excuses to stop loving their spouses because of their spouses' sins. But if this were a valid excuse, every one of us could avoid the call to love, since every one of us married a sinner!

One woman came up to me after a seminar and said, "It would be easy to be married if my husband were half as holy as you." I managed to contain my laughter and pointed out that she had no idea how "holy" I was; my wife feels pushed beyond her limit in many areas while trying to love this sinful man.

But that's not the point! I am not called to love my wife because she is holier than other wives (though I'm deeply thankful for her godliness). I am not called to love her because she makes me happy (though I am grateful for the many good times we share). I am not called to love her because she makes me go all gooey inside (though sometimes she still does). I am called to love her *out of reverence for God*. Any other motivation is less than Christian.

If I am to rid myself of anything that may contaminate body or spirit, then I can give no place in my life to jealousy, bitterness, resentment, or selfishness. I am always called to practice gentleness, kindness, goodness, faithfulness, and self-control. Someone else's sin — even the sin of my spouse against me — never gives me the license to respond with sin. I am called to just one motivation, and one only: reverence for God.

In one sense, what my spouse says or does or doesn't do is almost irrelevant. Every decision I make, every word I utter, every thought I think, every movement I perform, is to flow out of one holy motivation: reverence for God.

Are you a God-centered spouse?

2

A Prayer to Remember

Be imitators of God, therefore, as dearly loved children and live a life of love, just as Christ loved us and gave himself up for us as a fragrant offering and sacrifice to God.

Ephesians 5:1–2

When I come into town for "Sacred Marriage" seminars, I often get taken out to dinner beforehand. The organizers sometimes invite an engaged couple to join us. I always like this, particularly if I feel tired from traveling, because I know I can ask one question of the engaged woman that will reward me with a good rest. I know this because she will likely take at least ten minutes to answer. The question is this: "Tell me about your future husband."

The bride-to-be's eyes light up, and she starts to gush with enthusiastic and unqualified praise: "Oh, I so appreciate this about him, and he's so good at that, and he's so wonderfully thoughtful in this area, and in that area he's absolutely the best . . ."

Then, later in the weekend, I'll be with a group of wives and say, "Tell me about your husbands." I still get a rest, but I don't find it nearly as pleasant. The chorus goes like this: "He doesn't do this. He never does that. He wouldn't know how to *spell* 'spiritual leader,' much less act like one."

I go back to my hotel room and ask myself, "Where is the bridge that leads a woman to stop defining a man by what he *is* and start defining him by what he *is not?*"

The sad answer, unfortunately, is *marriage*. All our hopes, expectations, dreams, and ideals get poured into this real relationship. Because we marry a sinner, each day brings a new and often legitimate disappointment. Before long, we stop seeing what attracted us and instead become consumed by what disappoints us. Whereas before marriage our eyes filled with the glory of the person we had chosen to spend our lives with, now our eyes get filled only with their shortcomings.

I end the "Sacred Marriage" seminar with a story about a woman who decided to marry a man who was severely disabled in a work-related fire. While he could certainly offer emotional, relational, and spiritual support, such a man obviously will lack a lot of other things women typically seek.

"Ask yourself what a blind man with no arms and only one leg can't do for himself, much less for you," I'll say, "and then tell me what your husband *isn't*. Tell me how your wife disappoints you, or how your spouse doesn't live up to your highest ideals."

Every day, millions of couples wake up and evaluate their marriages by asking themselves, "Am I happier today than I was yesterday?" but I think there's a much better question we could ask. It comes from a song I heard on the radio, with one line that goes like this: "Ain't nobody gonna say good-bye, ain't nobody ever really tried to love you like I love you."

The poor grammar aside, there's some good theology in there. I'm called to love my wife like nobody ever has and nobody ever will. I am called to be the one person so devoted to her overall good that I commit myself to being there on her behalf, regardless of any disappointments or faults, so that on the day I die, while my wife may well remember the many bad habits I carried with me to my grave, she might yet say, "But you know what? That man loved me like I've never been loved; I can't imagine ever being loved like that again." If she can say this, then I'll know I've "succeeded" at this thing called marriage. It won't be about dying happier than other men; it'll be about whether I have truly loved.

So here's the question — more of a prayer, actually. Instead of waking up and asking yourself, "Am I happier today than I was yesterday?" how about praying, "Lord, how can I love my spouse today like she [or he] has never been or ever will be loved?"

You know what I've found? That's a prayer God *loves* to answer in very practical ways. He delights in loving his children, and he searches the earth to find someone willing to be his agent to fulfill this quest.

Just imagine how your marriage might change if, before your husband or wife returned home from work this evening, you spent some time asking God — and listening for his response — "Lord, how can I love him [or her] today like he [or she] has never been loved?" The answer may be very practical: take over a chore, speak a word of encouragement, take care of something that needs fixing. Or it may be romantic, or over-the-top creative, or generous, or very simple.

But ask God to help you. Partner with him to build up and encourage the person with whom you've chosen to spend the rest of your life.

Ask.

"How can I love my spouse today like he [or she] has never been or ever will be loved?"

When we focus on what *we* can do, it's amazing how little time we have left to become consumed by our disappointments.

3

Keeping the Focus
Where It Belongs

*"Why do you look at the speck of sawdust in your brother's eye
and pay no attention to the plank in your own eye? How can you say
to your brother, 'Brother, let me take the speck out of your eye,' when
you yourself fail to see the plank in your own eye? You hypocrite, first
take the plank out of your eye, and then you will see clearly to remove
the speck from your brother's eye."*

Luke 6:41–42

"Gary," the email read, "what does a wife do when her husband
doesn't love her like Christ loves the church?"

I responded by pointing out that no husband alive loves his wife
this well. While all Christian husbands should aspire to it, the truth
is that we all fall short.

I soon received a second email.

"Here's my story," she wrote. "Before I got married, I read ten
Harlequin romances a day, and I thought marriage would be like
that. For a while it was, but then things cooled off. A couple years
later, I found that exciting love once again by having an affair; but
after a number of months, that cooled off as well."

At that point, she had thrown herself into the church, but after
a while even God became boring. That's when she "fell" into yet
another affair, which — no surprise here — also eventually cooled off.
In the aftermath of those two affairs, in which she wounded and
humiliated her husband about as deeply as a wife can, she wrote to
me, consumed with how her husband wasn't loving her like Christ
loves the church.

Admittedly, this is an extreme example, but all of us have hearts
that tend toward dismissing our own faults while magnifying the

flaws of our spouses. Sometimes we need an extreme example to show us how dark our own hearts really are.

Jesus could not have been clearer: "Why do you look at the speck of sawdust in your brother's eye and pay no attention to the plank in your own eye? How can you say to your brother, 'Brother, let me take the speck out of your eye,' when you yourself fail to see the plank in your own eye? You hypocrite, first take the plank out of your eye, and then you will see clearly to remove the speck from your brother's eye" (Luke 6:41–42).

If you're thinking, "But in my case, my spouse really *is* the worst sinner," then know this: Jesus is talking specifically about *you*. This is precisely the attitude he finds so offensive.

Humans arguing about who is holier is like a couple of twenty-five handicap golfers fighting over which one of them can drive the ball farther — while Tiger Woods watches over their shoulder. We're all so many degrees below God's standard of perfection that even the holiest of humans is in desperate, aching need of God's gracious mercy and forgiveness.

While we tend to rank certain sins, in the glory of God's goodness every mark of sin — whether an errant attitude, a prideful spirit, or a lust of the flesh — is vile and offensive in his sight. I've seen wives who abuse food disdain husbands who struggle with pornography; I've seen controlling and arrogant husbands disdain wives who watch too much television. Both seem completely blinded to their own shortcomings.

We're not called to judge our spouses — ever; we are called to *love* them. We are not called to recount their failures in a Pharisaic game of "I'm holier than you"; we're called to *encourage* them. We are not called to build a case against them regarding how far they fall short of the glory of God; we are called to *honor and respect* them.

A final thought: You might never talk to another person about your spouse's weaknesses, but when you pray for or about him or her, how do you sound to God? Are you spending more time asking God how you can love your spouse like he or she has never been or ever will be loved, or are you endlessly repeating your spouse's failures and presenting God with a laundry list of things you want him to change?

If God seems silent, maybe he's hoping you'll catch a clue and turn the mirror on yourself. For the next week, revolutionize your marriage by asking God where *you* fall short. Every time you're tempted to turn the spotlight on your spouse, ask for God's gentle correction: "Lord, where am I falling short of your will for me to be a loving husband [a loving wife]? Where do I need to grow? Am I loving my spouse with the extravagant love displayed by Jesus?"

4

Growing Old Together

O LORD, you are my God;
I will exalt you and praise your name,
for in perfect faithfulness
you have done marvelous things.

Isaiah 25:1

Hollywood actor Al Pacino once talked about attending a Frank Sinatra concert in the early 1980s. When he arrived, he discovered that the opening act featured Buddy Rich, the famous drummer. Suddenly, it dawned on Al that Buddy was in his sixties — and he was going to play the drums? Al confessed, "I'm thinking, now I'm going to sit here and listen to him drum for a while and twiddle my thumbs until Frank Sinatra comes out."

And then something totally unexpected happened. Buddy Rich sat down and pulled sounds, rhythms, and cadences out of that set of instruments the likes of which Al Pacino had never heard. He sat mesmerized, confessing that Buddy Rich "transcended what I thought he was gonna do tenfold. And it became this *experience*."

Rich amazed the entire audience. Everyone stood up in unison and started screaming, at which point Frank Sinatra came out and said, "You see this guy drumming? You know, sometimes it's a good idea to stay at a thing." [1]

Sometimes it's a good idea to stay at a thing.

Persevering in a marriage creates something that nothing else can match. A deep marriage takes time to build, as well as tremendous effort, but something about a love that has endured surpasses even the thrill of newly discovered affection and infatuation. Hollywood likes to celebrate the couples who have just met and can't keep their hands off each other, who talk baby talk incessantly and practically smother each other with their affection. But Lisa and I have

developed a much greater appreciation for those couples in their sixties and seventies who have all but melted into each other.

A 1996 study in *Social Psychology Quarterly* found that the happiness of most couples declines somewhat for the first twenty years of
marriage, but those who make it to their thirty-fifth anniversary find
themselves as happy with each other as they felt when they were new-
lyweds. [2] Why is this so? Romance in the early years of marriage
quickly gets assaulted by unmet expectations, the duties of child rear-
ing, financial concerns, and the busyness of life. But during that emotional winter, unseen roots sink deep into the ground, ready to
produce a fruit that a new but untested love can never match. A certain intimacy begins to develop, provided we don't kill it with divorce.

I see this in my parents, and I see it in couples I don't even know.
You've seen them, too — in their seventies or eighties, frail creatures
physically but strong in love, who walk together as a unit. They've
become one in almost every sense of the word — in the way they
order their hamburgers, find a table, eat their lunch, and walk back
to their car. They have perfected the dance, and every step comes in
unison.

People who flit from relationship to relationship as their infatu-
ations lead them aren't really happy; they're desperate — and they'll
never find what they're looking for as they allow their desperation
to bury potential life partners. There is no perfect "soul mate," either
for them or for us. There will be only sinner after sinner after sinner.
But when you learn to accept and love one particular sinner over several decades, you can slowly build an alliance and intimacy that nothing else can match.

Love doesn't have to slowly fade away like a snowman on a
warm day. It can grow like an avalanche in power and force, picking
up strength along the way.

Sometimes it's a good idea to stay at a thing.

5

God's Son, God's Daughter

Can a mother forget the baby at her breast
and have no compassion on the child she has borne?
Though she may forget,
I will not forget you!
See, I have engraved you on the palms of my hands.

Isaiah 49:15–16

One day in prayer, I sensed that God was telling me very directly that Lisa wasn't just my wife; she's also his daughter, and I was to treat her accordingly.

This was a moment of revelation for me, and the force of this insight grew once I had kids of my own. If you want to get on my "good side," just be good to one of my kids. A wonderful young woman at our church became Allison's "big sister," taking her out to Starbucks or for ice cream and being a positive influence. And my wife and I will love Amy for the rest of our lives. Why? She was generous and kind to one of our children.

Conversely, if you really want to make me angry, pick on my kids. Be mean to them. Bully them. You'll fire up my righteous anger faster than anything you could possibly do to me.

So when I realized I am married to *God's daughter* — and that you, women, are married to *God's sons* — everything about how I view marriage changed overnight. It was no longer about just me and one other person; it was very much a relationship with a passionately interested third partner. We have been encouraged to contemplate the Fatherhood of God, a wonderful and true doctrine. But if you want to change your marriage, extend this analogy and spend some time thinking about God as Father-*in-Law*. Because he is!

When I fail to respect my wife — when I demean her or trouble her, when I'm condescending toward her or mistreat her in any way —

I am courting trouble with the heavenly Father, who feels passionately about my spouse's welfare.

Most of us fail to grasp just how fully God loves the person we married. Even if you were to spend ten years thinking about it, you'd still fall short of how much God truly cares about your spouse. He designed and created the person to whom you are married. He wooed him or her to regeneration. He adores and feels passionately about him or her. If any doubt remains as to his care and concern, consider this: he sent his Son to die on his or her behalf.

As the human father of three children, I fervently pray that each one of my children will marry a spouse who will love him or her generously and respect and enjoy him or her. I realize each of my children has certain quirks or limitations that might test a future spouse, but I pray that their spouses will be kind in these areas rather than use them to belittle my children or make them feel smaller. I hope with all my heart they'll find partners who will encourage them with a gracious spirit. I pray they won't marry someone who will be stingy or selfish or who might abuse them. I know my kids aren't perfect — but I want them to have spouses who will love them despite their imperfections.

In the same way, God is fully aware of our spouses' limitations — and he is just as eager for us to be kind and generous with these faults as we are for our kids' future spouses to be kind to them.

Think about how you treated your husband or wife this past week — is that how you want your son or daughter to be treated by his or her spouse? Never forget: you didn't just marry a man or a woman; you married God's son or God's daughter.

Treat him, treat her, accordingly.

6

The Gift of Fear

I feared the anger and wrath of the LORD.

Deuteronomy 9:19

If I could preach only one sermon to the church today, it wouldn't be about faith. We hear more about faith today than ever before in the history of the church.

It would be about fear.

Moses felt motivated by a godly fear of a holy God: "I feared the anger and wrath of the LORD" (Deuteronomy 9:19). According to the book of Isaiah, Jesus had more than mere wisdom and understanding and knowledge; he also lived with a healthy fear of the Lord (Isaiah 11:2–3).

Biblical fear is more complex and profound than what we usually think of when we use the English word *fear*. It isn't defined fully by the words *terror* and *dread*. Although it encompasses these emotions, it also carries the idea of a passionate love, the positive desire to please God, and a worshipful awe.[3]

God is gracious—yes! God is merciful—absolutely! God is kind and good and loving and caring—no doubt! But it is still a fearful thing to offend God, to fall into his holy hands, for he is a just God with the power and might and will to carry out judgments against those who offend him. Our Lord used this godly fear to root the early church in a proper attitude toward him. Ananias and Sapphira lost their lives when they tried to deceive the apostolic leaders. The surviving community responded just as God intended: "Great fear seized the whole church and all who heard about these events" (Acts 5:11). Keep in mind, this is the church *after* Pentecost, filled with the Holy Spirit but still needing an appropriate fear to help its members live godly lives.

How does this relate to marriage? It's directly tied to last week's devotion. Your heavenly Father-in-Law never takes his eyes off his beloved child. He hears every word uttered in anger toward his children. He sees every act of violence; he witnesses every act of denial, manipulation, and control. Never imagine that he witnesses such assaults with a dispassionate apathy; on the contrary, he feels each slight as though you were persecuting Christ himself.

That's the truth of Acts 9. Saul thought he was persecuting the Christians, but Jesus made it very personal: "'Who are you, Lord?' Saul had asked after Jesus called out to him. 'I am Jesus, whom you are persecuting'" (Acts 9:5).

You didn't marry an orphan; you married a man or woman with a very influential, very powerful, and all-seeing Dad. Based on how you're loving and caring for your spouse, how happy do you think your heavenly Father-in-Law feels with you? Is he smiling over your extravagant love? Or are you storing up his anger and wrath because of how you're mistreating his precious son or daughter?

I fully realize that talking about the fear of God seems outdated. Recently a pastor told me outright he didn't believe he should "fear" God but rather "love" him. And yet the Bible is clear that "[the church] was strengthened; and encouraged by the Holy Spirit, it grew in numbers, living in the fear of the Lord" (Acts 9:31).

Listen, I adore God. I feel safe with him. But I also fear him. The biggest changes in my marriage have come from listening to God in prayer, from being chastised and rebuked and encouraged directly by him. Most of us know by now that physical attraction won't hold a marriage together. We also realize that the trials of living with a sinner will, in time, temper our romantic affection.

But the fear of God—that's eternal. That lasts. That's a solid foundation on which to build a lifelong marriage. God hears every conversation. He sees every act of every day. He even reads our thoughts. I might be three thousand miles away from my wife, far from her sight, but the God before whom I promised I'd be faithful is in that hotel room with me.

I've come to view the fear of God as a shelter, a covering, a mighty force. I know I'm sinful. I know my own good intentions are far too weak in the face of way too many temptations. I've broken promises before, so I know I can break them again. But I've also found that my fear of God is growing greater than my rebellion; it reins in my baser instincts. It helps me to make choices that lead me to become the type of man I want to be rather than the type of man I despise.

I can't imagine living a single day without the fear of the Lord — and there's no way I could contemplate trying to be married without that same covering. The best gift you can give your spouse is to fear the God who made him or her. That's a gift that *truly* keeps on giving.

Don't Look Back

Therefore, if anyone is in Christ, he is a new creation; the old has gone, the new has come!

2 Corinthians 5:17

A relationship from my teen years still makes me wince whenever the girl's name comes to mind and I think about the hurt I caused her. One day recently I was wondering and praying about looking her up to tell her how sorry I felt for how I acted twenty-five years ago.

One of my best friends — a marriage and family therapist from San Diego — adamantly opposed the idea. "Gary," Steve said, "I'm thinking this is more about you than it is about her." In his counseling experience, Steve has discovered that looking up someone after two and a half decades can be dangerous; you don't know where he or she is coming from or what's happening in his or her life. The potential for hurt is just as great as the potential for healing.

But the clincher came when he said, "Look, why don't you take all the energy you're using thinking about this and spend it on planning how you can love your wife *today?*"

That's when it dawned on me: Guilt attacks us by using a dead relationship to distract us from a living one.

I remember the time a woman approached me after I had taught on the topic of sacred history — the meaning two people build together when they persevere through the difficult seasons in life. After hearing me talk, she felt convinced she had sought an unbiblical divorce with her first husband — but it was too late to go back. She had remarried and her ex-husband had remarried, and now she was poisoning her current marriage with the dead relationship from the past.

"The real danger here," I said, "is that through this guilt about the past, you'll fail to love your second husband, just like you failed your first husband. It seems to me your charge is to focus on loving your current husband like he's never been or ever will be loved. You need to stop thinking about your first husband, and focus on the husband you're called to love *now*."

I saw a light go on in her countenance when I said this — and I could see visible relief on her second husband's face. Clearly, he had been feeling cheated.

Some things in our past can't be "fixed." You can repent, you can ask for forgiveness; but you can't always go back — nor should you try. Some of us are more introspective and hold on to our guilt in such a way that we become blinded to our present obligations.

When guilt comes knocking on your door about a failed relationship from the past, start praying about how to love your spouse today. Don't let a dead relationship pollute or weigh down a living one.

For others, the dead relationship isn't about guilt but about fantasy. These folks allow a relationship that never worked out to steal the energy they should be pouring into their marriage. "If only I had married him instead!" they think, or, "I wonder what so-and-so is doing right now?" So instead of praying about how to love his or her spouse, he or she daydreams about being married to this other person.

There are few things so destructive and self-defeating as giving way to such fantasies — fantasies that can't be fulfilled in a biblically appropriate way. Since there's little chance this relationship can happen (I've even heard people confess they've tried to justify these thoughts by wondering what might happen if their current spouse died), it is simply wasted time — time stolen from what you could be using to make your current marriage more meaningful.

Besides, there's a reason behind why this dead relationship isn't a living one! Our memories tend to be very selective. We forget the negative and fixate on the positive — and every such fantasy robs our spouses of energy and thought that should be expended on them.

Don't look back. You're cheating your spouse — and ultimately yourself — when you do. Pour all your energy into something current and real.

Fame Is Trumped by Intimacy

*I belong to my lover,
and his desire is for me.*

Song of Songs 7:10

John Wooden is the undisputed best at what he did. You can debate the greatest college football coach of all time; you can debate the best professional basketball coach. But there's no debating the best college basketball coach of all time.

It's John Wooden, hands down.

Wooden's UCLA Bruins won ten NCAA championships. No other coach has won more than four. In an incredible three-and-a-half-year run, his Bruins went undefeated for eighty-eight straight games. Now that it seems as though twelve-year-olds are entering the NBA draft, it's highly unlikely any other coach will ever have a program stable enough to match that string.

Wooden retired in 1975 but remains so respected that he can hardly enter a room without getting a standing ovation. Many publishers would eagerly throw a six-figure contract at him if he would write another book. He could command speaking fees in the tens of thousands.

But Coach Wooden has his eyes on something other than popular acclaim. Rick Reilly, a writer for *Sports Illustrated*, paid Coach Wooden a visit and soon found himself in something of an awkward situation. How do you tactfully tell a man in his nineties that you hope he doesn't die because this world still needs him and there's nobody else like him waiting in the wings?

Coach Wooden picked up on Rick's message and finally said, "I'm not afraid to die. Death is my only chance to be with her again."[4]

The "her" John referred to was his wife, Nellie, who died in 1985 after fifty-three years of marriage. John is still very connected to this woman. On the twenty-first of every month, he writes a passionate letter to Nellie, telling her how much he misses her, loves her, and values the time they had together. Then he folds the letter and puts it on a pile near where he sleeps.

That stack now has over two hundred letters.

By his own admission, John would gladly leave this world of acclaim if in doing so he could be reunited with the love of his life.

I don't believe I'm insulting you by saying you'll never achieve the acclaim of John Wooden. You may be very, very good at what you do — but can you ever honestly hope to be considered the absolute best of anyone who has ever pursued your profession?

So often, we ignore our marriages in pursuit of high acclaim — but John Wooden, a man who received that acclaim, would gladly give it up for more time with his wife: "I'm not afraid to die. Death is my only chance to be with her again."

Sadly, many of us learn this lesson too late. We spend our entire lives ignoring the glory and power of true love and intimacy with one person for the elusive elixir of fame. Let's learn a lesson from a man who has been there — who has seen both sides and who remains convinced that a relationship with a spouse who truly knows you and loves you and who walks with you is far more fulfilling to the soul than receiving applause from the crowd or adoration from afar.

Of course, most of us won't even smell national acclaim. Even so, we shortchange our spouses for something much smaller: a corner office, a pay raise, the esteem of our neighborhood friends, two strokes off our golf handicap, fear that others will look down on our family-centered lifestyle . . .

If you're a wife, you may be chided for showing such concern and attention to your husband. It's certainly out of fashion to even think about being a devoted wife. Just witness the controversy surrounding the release of Dr. Laura Schlessinger's book *The Proper Care and Feeding of Your Husband*. Some will mock you for "degrading" yourself and urge you to "get your own life."

And yet, if you will ignore this disdain and truly dedicate yourself to loving this man, you will receive far more in the end than you ever will from others' approval. Consider the poem "To Her Loving Husband," written by the Puritan wife Anne Bradstreet:

If ever two were one, then surely we.
If ever man were lov'd by wife, then thee;

If ever wife was happy in a man,
Compare with me, ye women, if you can.[5]

Have any of your mockers ever felt such a sentiment about their husbands? Have they ever known such a love?

You can.

Go for something real. Develop an appetite for authentic intimacy. Dive into your marriage, and discover the quiet but profound pleasure of loving and being loved, of truly knowing and being known. To be loved well and to be known completely by one is far more fulfilling than being adored by many and truly known by none.

9

A Soul Filled with God

One thing I ask of the LORD,
this is what I seek:
that I may dwell in the house of the LORD
all the days of my life,
to gaze upon the beauty of the LORD
and to seek him in his temple.

Psalm 27:4

Personal worship is an absolute necessity for a strong marriage. It comes down to this: If I stop receiving from God, I start demanding from others. Instead of appreciating and loving and serving others, I become disappointed in them. Instead of cherishing my wife, I become aware of her shortcomings. I take out my frustrations with a less-than-perfect life and somehow blame *her* for my lack of fulfillment.

But when my heart gets filled by God's love and acceptance, I'm set free to love instead of worrying about being loved. I'm motivated to serve instead of becoming obsessed about whether I'm being served. I'm moved to cherish instead of feeling unappreciated.

Madeleine complains about a lack of spiritual intimacy in her relationship with her husband, Martin. "He's never been what you might call a spiritual leader," she says, and this has become almost an obsession for her — as though her own spiritual health depends on her husband suddenly becoming mature.

"Did Teresa of Avila have a spiritual leader?" I asked her. "Madame Guyon? Mother Teresa of Calcutta? What about the countless widows who now pursue God on their own? Were — and are — their lives empty simply because they aren't married to a spiritually mature man?"

Tim is upset because his wife never initiates physical intimacy. Like Madeleine, he's become fixated on one issue in his marriage, so that he can hardly even pray — which makes him feel even more emotionally dependent on the sexual intimacy he's not getting. "Tim," I said, "I remember praying with a husband whose wife was in the last stages of severe multiple sclerosis. It had been years since they could enjoy anything even approximating normal sexual relations. Do you think God has wired this world in such a way that her husband has no chance to be happy and fulfilled because his wife can't initiate — or even perform?"

Tim had expected me to preach only to his wife, not to him. "In fact," I added, "he found great joy in taking care of her — and that meant cleaning out a bedpan on a regular basis."

Certainly, spiritual intimacy and sexual relations are legitimate desires, but you know what? Whenever I place my happiness in the hands of another human being, I'm virtually guaranteeing some degree of disappointment. It can be as frivolous as a barista not getting my chai at Starbucks just the way I like it, or it can be as profound as some pastor I really admire falling into sin.

That's why worship sets me free. It meets my most basic need — to rest in the fact that I am known and loved, that I have a purpose, and that my eternal destiny and delight are secure — so that lesser needs (including spiritual companionship and sexual desires) serve the role of an occasional dessert rather than my main meal.

It's simply not fair to ask your spouse to fulfill you. No one can. If you expect your spouse to be God for you, your spouse will fail every day and on every account. Not only that, should your disappointment lead you to divorce, your second, third, and even fourth spouses will fail you too!

Only one can love you like God, with a perfect, constantly steady, and giving love — and that is God himself. When the "one thing" we seek is to dwell in God's house, to gaze upon his beauty, and to seek him in his temple, our soul's sense of desperate need is met in our heavenly Father's arms. Then we leave this temple and find tremendous joy in giving, in loving, and in serving rather than in keeping close accounts as to whether we're being loved or being served.

Maybe it's just me, but I've seen a constant formula at work in my life: the less I receive from God, the more I demand from my wife; the more I receive from God, the more I am set free to give to my wife.

The best thing you can do for your marriage is to fill your soul with God. Start defining disappointment with your spouse as spiritual hunger, a cosmic call to worship. Marriage is a wonderful institution, but it is limited. It can't replace God. Don't ask it to.

The Foundation of Fellowship

But if we walk in the light, as he is in the light, we have fellow-ship with one another, and the blood of Jesus, his Son, purifies us from all sin.

1 John 1:7

An actress who once had one of the most popular shows on cable television wrote a sex manual with her husband, praising him as an "artist" and liberally sharing the delight the two of them experienced in bed.

Barely a year after the book came out, the actress announced that she and her husband had separated. Later, the two divorced.

Couples won't save their marriages by becoming athletes in bed. They won't stave off divorce by increasing their income. They won't find that having children will reinvigorate a dead marriage. All these efforts have been tried and found wanting, because what most frustrated marriages lack is what the Bible calls *fellowship*.

I know, fellowship sounds like a pretty mundane word. How can fellowship ever hope to compete with sex?

It doesn't have to. That's the beauty of Christian marriage: we can completely embrace the intoxicating pleasure of physical passion, while also appreciating the profound but quieter fulfillment of fellowship.

God made us social beings, and a lot of couples do "social" things: go out to dinner, watch a movie or television, take a vacation, and, yes, have sex. But these social things fall short of the biblical meaning of fellowship. What often gets left behind is the deeply meaningful interaction between two believers, both filled with the Holy Spirit, who encourage each other by their mutual passion for God and who use their God-given spiritual gifts to build each other up as together they seek first the kingdom of God.

This is the heart of biblical fellowship. It is sharing spiritual struggles, being open to loving confrontation and rebuke, and submitting ourselves to the correction of God's Word, appropriately applied. It is praying for and with each other. It is encouraging each other to fully use the gifts God has given us, testifying to the risen Christ through his work in our bodies. It is cultivating *together* an increased passion for God. Such a fellowship will maintain loyalty between the peaks of physical passion.

I have been married for almost two decades now, and the longer I'm married, the more convinced I become that my primary relationship with Lisa — even above being married to her — is as her brother in Christ. This is an eternal bond we'll share for the next ten million years (and beyond). As her brother in the Lord, I am committed to her well-being, even apart from how we are doing in our marriage. I want the best for her. I want her to grow in holiness — not so *my* life will be easier (God's work in her may, in fact, inconvenience me), but so she will surrender to God's will for her life.

When our marriages have an empty spiritual core, we put too much emphasis on things that can't sustain or nurture a marriage — like sex. Sex is a wonderful gift, but it can't fill an empty spiritual core. The emphasis we place on it can be almost comical. Here's an example: Lisa and I love to go on walks in the woods; it's one of our favorite things to do together. It would never occur to me after such a walk to immediately pelt Lisa with the question, "So, was that an especially good walk?"

"What are you talking about?"

"Well, was that walk as good for you as it was for me?"

"Gary, have you lost your mind?"

"I want to know! Was that walk better than the last walk? Was it maybe the best walk you've ever had?"

Such talk would cheapen an activity we greatly enjoy doing together, and it would put absurd pressure on each episode.

Without a strong spiritual core, we give certain activities an emphasis they don't deserve, while ignoring the things that really do create long-term intimacy.

Improving your skills in bed may have its place, but good sex alone won't create a good marriage, and good sex doesn't necessarily — by any means — lead to better fellowship. On the other hand, strong fellowship almost always leads to better sex. Sex is, inherently, a spiritual activity, even though it is expressed in very physical terms. In his book *Sex, Romance, and the Glory of God*, C. J. Mahaney puts it this way:

> When Carolyn and I are behind closed doors and locked in a passionate embrace, that moment is either enhanced or diminished by how well I have been leading in the area of loving communication. So, to talk about romantic communication and creativity is not to delay talking about sex. It is to talk about what makes for the best sex. Communication and sex are inseparable. It's not as though sex is one thing and communication is something else. Life doesn't divide up into neat little compartments like that, especially in the oneness of marriage. It's all one thing.[6]

Most of us don't need to spice up our marriages so much as we need to dig deeper in the Lord. Are you asking your sexual relationship to compensate for a lack of spiritual intimacy? That's backwards! Spend some time this week thinking about how the two of you can better express what it means to be a brother and sister in the Lord. How can you pray for each other? How can you share more honestly and more intimately? How can you encourage each other in your individual passion for God?

Nothing else on this earth rivals the inner satisfaction of a relationship built on biblical fellowship.

11

The Heart To

Above all else, guard your heart,
for it is the wellspring of life.

Proverbs 4:23

Mark, a Midwestern family physician with a good eye for investments, has lifted his family into affluence through hard work. He's provided his wife — who comes from a poorer background — with a good living, and he's the type of husband who does the dishes, puts the kids to bed while his wife reads or takes a bath, and is the first to volunteer for "car duty" (taking the kids to their sporting and church events).

Because of his job, Mark needs to literally leave the city to get away from his work — otherwise, someone stops him after church to ask about a sore shoulder or an irregular heartbeat. At the grocery store, he can be asked to diagnose a rash, and at the library he might be stopped to give his opinion on a daily aspirin regimen that someone just heard mentioned on the radio.

More than anything, Mark appreciates getting away with his wife, so the two of them can enjoy each other's company without interruption. It would mean even more to him if his wife would plan a weekend, or even just a night away, six to eight times a year. It's not as though Charlotte (Mark's wife) isn't equipped to handle this. Before the investments came in, she used to work in the travel industry; but she now has the opportunity to do basically whatever she wants.

Even so, by the time I spoke with Mark, it had been almost a year since Charlotte had planned anything like this. Mark reminds Charlotte of this every five months or so, which usually results in a heated argument that ends with Charlotte saying, "Fine, go get your calendar and we'll plan something right now."

"That *really* makes me want to get away," Mark says sarcastically.

While how-to marriage books and seminars certainly have their value and place, on their own they miss the key issue. It's not really about *how* to; far more often, it's about whether we have the *heart* to. Charlotte knows how to please her husband; she just lacks the heart to do it.

Motivation is more than half the battle. You don't have to teach an infatuated couple how to communicate. Infatuated couples don't read books about resolving disputes; they don't watch instructional videos about making time for each other. Why not? Because when you possess the heart to do these things, the how-to takes care of itself.

If the two of you used to communicate, used to keep romance alive, used to find ways to maintain intimacy in spite of differing opinions, that's evidence enough that, somewhere, you already possess these basic skills. It's not like you lost the skills you had as a younger man or woman. The real issue is whether you're willing to exercise those skills.

If I have the heart to romance my wife, I'll find a way to romance her. I was great at romancing her twenty years ago. In fact, I wrote her cards and letters, taped little notes around her room, planned creative dates — the works. Now, in my forties, do I have fewer romance skills than I possessed in my twenties?

Of course not. The real issue is, do I have less heart for such activities in my forties than I had in my twenties? Am I acting "out of reverence for God" (2 Corinthians 7:1), pursuing Lisa just as aggressively out of a motivation of faith as formerly I felt motivated by mere emotion? Or am I allowing daily duties to take time and energy away from loving my wife?

Charlotte knows she is married to a loving, godly man who is a good provider. She also knows he doesn't ask much in return — but she has lost the heart to give him even that. She knows how to plan an outing, but for whatever reason, she has lost the will.

In the same way, most wives know what their husbands want. Most have a basic understanding of how to please him. That's not to say you can't pick up a few helpful tips along the way, but you know most of what you need to know to make your husband a satisfied spouse. The real question is, do you have the heart to do what you know how to do?

Sometimes, we hide behind the how-to because it doesn't feel as shameful as purposefully withholding on our spouses. Men say, "I don't know how to romance my wife. After all, I'm a guy!" But what we really mean is, "It's more acceptable to play the 'stupid male' role than to admit I'm so self-centered that I fail to take the time to show my wife how much I cherish her."

Can I challenge you to spend just as much time examining your heart as you do filling your head? Will you sit before the Lord for as long as you pore over the latest self-help book? Will you allow the Holy Spirit to convict, instruct, chasten, and encourage?

Be quiet throughout this week. Listen to the Lord's still, small voice. Let him name your true motivation. I hope those motivations will be charity, kindness, goodwill, patience, and love. But mixed in with such attitudes may be spite, bitterness, resentment, selfishness, or sheer laziness. Ask the Lord to show you where you're withholding on your spouse. Let him hold up a mirror to your heart's true condition.

Keep in mind that it's not as though the heart is ever fixed once and for all. While I may have the "heart to" today, it doesn't guarantee I'll have the "heart to" tomorrow. We need to regularly examine our hearts.

Listen: when we first laid eyes on our spouses and decided to make them ours, we found a way to attract and maintain their attention. We had far less knowledge of our spouses then than we have today — but we also had the heart then, and that made all the difference. If you've fallen into a silent season, nine times out of ten it's an issue of the heart, not of a lack of knowledge.

Fire up that will! Let God charge your motivation. You already know most of what you need to know. Now, you just have to get busy doing it. What one thing can you do today?

12

The Preyer

Be self-controlled and alert. Your enemy the devil prowls around like a roaring lion looking for someone to devour.

1 Peter 5:8

Previous generations of Christians may have paid too much attention to the devil, but our age tends to pay him too little heed. The severe truth is that Satan hates your marriage and makes its destruction a nearly daily aim.

It is said that while Francis of Assisi prayed for his Order, "by divine revelation he saw the whole Place surrounded and besieged by devils, as by a great army." Much to Francis's satisfaction, the demons couldn't find a place to enter, until one of the friars was stirred to anger and began to plot revenge on a brother. "As a result, the gate of virtue being abandoned and the door of wickedness being open, he gave the devil a way to come in."[7]

Francis called for the offending brother and confronted him. The brother confessed that he had, indeed, been making vengeful plans; he repented, and the gate to hell slammed shut.

While many today might snicker at such a "primitive" worldview presented in a classic book written almost seven hundred years ago, our modern naïveté concerning spiritual realities is at least as pathetic. When we quarrel with each other; hold resentments; allow bitterness to simmer; play petty games of control, manipulation, and revenge, we do, in fact, open up the door to spiritual beings who seek to destroy the holy family God has called us to create.

Jesus taught constant vigilance when he told his disciples how to pray. The Lord's Prayer includes these words: "And lead us not into temptation, but deliver us from the evil one" (Matthew 6:13). Notice, Jesus didn't say, "deliver us from evil" but from "the evil one." Jesus told his followers to regularly petition God so that they wouldn't fall prey to the evil one's schemes.

A married couple's relationship is the inner fortress in a cosmic spiritual battle. This fortress is not limited to just a man and woman; it also protects the children who result from that union. Even more than that, it protects generations of grandchildren and great-grandchildren, who will be influenced by their ancestors.

With so much at stake, can we afford to be lackadaisical? Dare we forget that a powerful, pernicious being has made it his aim to wreck what God is trying to build? Even worse, are we cooperating with his agenda? By our actions, whether physical (flirting with an office mate, viewing pornography, getting so busy we have little or no time to work on our marriages) or spiritual (refusing to forgive, holding a grudge, neglecting to build spiritual intimacy), are we foolishly and recklessly putting our marriages at risk?

Because Satan exists, we must remain vigilant over our souls and our relationships and refuse to provide any open doors that can invite Satan to work his wiles. One "little" thing, left untended, can be nursed and built up to become a major issue.

Flush out all of it today. Ask God to give you a forgiving heart, a loving heart, and a pure heart. Keep moving toward your spouse. Ask God to close any doors you have foolishly left open. Guard what God has given you; give Satan no place to enter.

Love Mercy

Love mercy.
Micah 6:8

A couple asked to speak to me after a "Sacred Marriage" seminar. The husband had done some truly heinous things, and their marriage seemed on the verge of breaking up. The wife rightfully desired to call him to account. We talked for over an hour, and both of them left in tears — good tears that were bringing healing and restoration.

I gave the sermon at their church the next morning, and the husband sheepishly approached me after the services. "I bet I'm the worst man you've ever preached to," he said.

"You've certainly done some awful things," I admitted, "and you and your wife invited me into some of your worst moments — but I know that's not the whole story. If someone created a video of *my* worst moments, and that's all you were to see about me, you'd be tempted to kick me out of this church before you'd shake my hand."

Because we married a sinner, we're going to see some ugly, ugly things. That's why our attitude toward another's sin will determine, in large part, the degree of intimacy we can achieve in marriage. A Pharisee might impress a mate, but he'll never get truly close to her, because judgment repels intimacy as surely as heat melts ice.

One glorious day, God used a Bible verse to open my eyes to a reality so large that it changed everything about how I view my marriage and my standing before God, as well as how I am to treat others. Micah 6:8 tell us to "love mercy." That short phrase — "love mercy" — kept playing in my mind.

Love mercy. Micah isn't telling us merely to "demonstrate" mercy or only to "practice" mercy; he tells us to fall in love with it!

The wide, biblical concept of mercy includes forgiveness but also has roots in loyalty. One commentator notes, "This steady, persistent refusal of God to wash his hands of wayward Israel is the essential meaning of the Hebrew word which is translated loving-kindness [or mercy]."[8] This is a loyalty and forgiveness seasoned with graciousness and kindness — particularly to those who don't deserve it. It is one of the most beautiful words in the English language and certainly one of the most precious truths in the Christian faith.

What does it mean to fall in love with mercy? It means I am to become mercy's biggest fan. Having received mercy from God, I am to walk in assurance and thankfulness, using my own gift of mercy as the lens through which I view anyone else's sin — including that of my spouse.

Mercy is wonderful. Without mercy, I'd be damned for all eternity. Through his mercy, God made a way for me to enjoy eternal happiness instead of never-ending pain and torture. Mercy also allows me to minister. As a fallen man who sins daily, I could never even begin to reach out to others with God's perfect gospel unless every hour I live in the joy of knowing that Jesus Christ's sacrifice on my behalf has set me free and washed me clean. In short, without mercy, I'd be toast; but with mercy, the celebratory toast never ends!

Falling in love with mercy means I love everything about it. It means I also love the way it applies to the person I married. Just as I love my wife when she's in the kitchen, the living room, and the bedroom, so I love mercy when it's applied to me, my wife, and my children. There is no arena where I don't delight in mercy. People who love mercy feel eager to show mercy to others. Like God, they not only *want* to forgive, they are *eager* to forgive. You don't have to convince them to show mercy; they love to show mercy!

A Christian spouse who understands mercy is a husband or wife who looks forward to another opportunity to demonstrate God's grace. It is a believer eager to forgive, whose first thought leaps toward reconciliation rather than revenge. Mercy isn't an obligation grudgingly given in to — it's the love of his or her life! It's his or her favorite practice.

Listen to one of the most practical applications of mercy I've ever read about. A wife got in an accident while driving a brand-new car. She felt understandably upset, fretting about what her husband would say when he found out. As she retrieved the insurance papers from the glove compartment, she found this note in her husband's handwriting: "Dear Mary, when you need these papers, remember it's you I love, not the car."[9]

You are an imperfect, very fallible, prone-to-mess-up sinner saved by mercy. You married a fallible sinner who needs the same remedy. The intimacy of marriage cannot be sustained without mercy. Our sin and guilt are so powerful that, absent mercy, every human relationship will fall before their might. You can self-righteously judge every spouse who has ever lived. You can prove his or her guilt in a court of law. You can compellingly state your case and clearly demonstrate how far your spouse has fallen short — but the judgment you render will kill intimacy in your own life; it won't kill sin in your spouse's life. It will also herald your spiritual poverty and destruction: "Judgment without mercy will be shown to anyone who has not been merciful. Mercy triumphs over judgment!" (James 2:13).

This week, meditate on mercy. Fall in love with it. Seek to understand what a gift you've been given in God's mercy. And then, from that foundation, explore the riches of extending this same mercy to others, beginning with your spouse. Commit to memory the theologically crucial phrase "Mercy triumphs over judgment," and seek to build your marriage anew on the back of God's gift rather than on the failed policies of the legalistic Pharisees.

One Bad Habit

Be perfect, therefore, as your heavenly Father is perfect.

Matthew 5:48

I wasn't happy with my wife.

Our family had talked about observing Lent, and without a moment's hesitation, both Lisa and my son, Graham, had it planned for me: "You need to give up Pepsi."

What, they think I couldn't do it? What is Lent — forty-six days? (We don't observe Lent like the Roman Catholics, who get to imbibe on Sunday; our family goes for an "absolute" Lent, from Ash Wednesday all the way up to Easter morning.) I could handle six and a half weeks, no problem.

Two weekends into the ordeal, I called Lisa from the Chicago airport. "Look," I complained, "I don't have a lot of diversions on the road. I don't look at *Playboy*. I don't rent dirty movies at the hotel. I don't get drinks at the bar. I don't even enjoy the occasional cigar on the golf course. What's so bad about a daily Pepsi? Why did you say I should give that up?"

"Those drinks are so bad for you," Lisa answered.

"Can't I have just one stinking vice?" I protested. "Just one?! You encouraged me to give up the one thing I can enjoy when I'm traveling and tired and stuck in an airport. Thanks a lot."

But you know what? Forty-six days later, after breaking the habit, I realized I really don't need a daily Pepsi. And how pathetic, anyway, that I count my one pleasure on the road sitting down with a sugary soft drink to get a caffeine pick-me-up? Breaking away from that "one stinking vice" helped me see that, in the long run, I might feel a lot better if I occasionally settled for an iced tea.

Admittedly, whether I drink a daily Pepsi is a very trivial matter — but the principle behind it goes much deeper. My statement

"Can't I have just one stinking vice?" has infected my own and many other marriages on a much more significant and profound level. Husbands may say, "Look, I don't have affairs. I don't gamble with the mortgage money. I'm home in the evening. Yeah, I occasionally lose my temper and wound you with a few careless words, but am I not allowed one vice?"

Wives may say, "I've been a faithful wife. I don't bust the family budget. I'm there for my family. Maybe at times I talk negatively about my husband behind his back when he really ticks me off, but all in all, I think he has it pretty good."

And so we excuse something we know we should change, but we ignore it, based on the faulty assumption that, since we are generally good husbands and wives, we can maintain our "one little vice."

But the Bible doesn't give us permission to ignore "one little vice." Second Corinthians 7:1 urges us to "purify ourselves from *everything* that contaminates body and spirit, perfecting holiness out of reverence for God" (emphasis added). When we say, "All in all, my spouse has it OK," we're not perfecting holiness; we're excusing wickedness.

I have a tendency to get a little short with my wife when a publishing deadline approaches — and this book was no exception. Just days before my editor needed the manuscript, Lisa and I had a misunderstanding, to which I responded in a less-than-gracious manner. I can excuse these episodes with, "Well, I'm under a lot of pressure right now, so it's to be expected," or I can take the attitude of perfecting holiness, resolving that I don't want to treat my wife like that — *ever*. Being generally gracious to her during the eleven and a half months of the year where I'm free of a deadline (not that I always am) doesn't mean I've stored up the right to neglect her or get short with her for those other two weeks. Instead, I can learn to recognize the temptation and more effectively prepare to deal with the stress in a way that won't wound my wife.

We fail to see that one hole can sink a ship as effectively as can ten holes; it may take a little longer, but the ship will still sink. Since any hole can threaten a marriage, such cavalier thinking has to be challenged.

The truth is, I'm *not* granted "one little vice." Jesus said, "Be perfect, therefore, as your heavenly Father is perfect" (Matthew 5:48). If something injures my relationship with Lisa, out of love I will work with God's Spirit to root that habit out of my life. I won't make excuses by pointing to the lack of other negative things about me, and I won't try to hide behind my strengths. A weakness is a weakness, regardless of any strengths that surround it. Sin is sin, regardless of how many virtues accompany it.

Doing good doesn't create marital "bank deposits" that allow us to make vice-ridden "withdrawals." Don't excuse that one little vice. Keep in mind that, apart from Christ's sacrifice, just "one little vice" would keep you out of heaven for all eternity.

This week, stop yourself when you start making excuses or try to explain away personality faults by thinking, "All in all, my spouse has it pretty good." Instead, challenge yourself with Scripture: "Be perfect, therefore, as your heavenly Father is perfect."

Soul Mate or Sole Mate?

Greater love has no one than this, that he lay down his life for his friends.

John 15:13

Well over two thousand years ago, the Greek philosopher Plato surmised that a perfect human being was tragically split in two, resulting in a race of creatures sentenced to spend the rest of their lives searching for that missing other who can complete them.

Thus was created the notion of the "soul mate."

Despite its bizarre historical underpinnings, the notion of a soul mate has rooted itself in our culture, inspiring countless movies, novels, and Top 40 songs. One Rutgers University study found that 94 percent of people in their twenties say that the first requirement in a spouse is being such a soul mate. Just as surprising, 87 percent think they'll actually find that person "when they are ready."[10] A culture suspicious of God has nevertheless brazenly embraced some sort of forceful and intelligent destiny that brings two lovelorn souls together!

But there's a danger in this line of thinking. Many people mistake a storm of emotion as the identifying mark of their soul mate. A student of my friend Byron Weathersbee once declared that she wanted to marry a man because "he gives me butterflies."

While we may laugh at this, I've seen far too many couples want to end a marriage simply because the butterflies have left. Individuals captivated by the "soul mate" line of thinking marry on an infatuation binge without seriously considering character, compatibility, life goals, family desires, spiritual health, and other important concerns. Then when the music fades and the relationship requires work, one or both partners suddenly discover that they were "mistaken": this person must not be their soul mate after all! Otherwise, it wouldn't be so much work. Next they panic. Their soul mate must still be out there! Such people can't get to divorce court fast enough, lest someone steal their "one true soul mate" meant only for them.

When we get married for trivial reasons, we tend to seek divorce for trivial reasons.

Can I suggest a more biblical pattern? Instead of following Plato in a wild pursuit of our soul mate, we should seek to find a biblical "sole mate." A sole mate is someone who willingly does the shoe-leather application of living out biblical love. The most accurate definition of true love is found in John 15:13: "Greater love has no one than this, that he lay down his life for his friends."

This love isn't based on feelings but on sacrifice. It pictures love, not as an emotion, but as a policy — a commitment we choose to keep. Such a love is not based on the worthiness of the person being loved — none of us deserve Christ's sacrifice! — but on the worthiness of the One who calls us to love: "We love because [God] first loved us" (1 John 4:19). This takes us back to the very first devotion: loving our spouses "out of reverence for God" (2 Corinthians 7:1).

A "sole mate" appreciates the truth that marriage is a school of character. He cherishes his spouse as an imperfect sister in Christ who is helping him develop the biblical skill of love. Clement of Alexandria, an early church father (ca. 150–215), captures this thinking marvelously when he writes, "The prize in the contest of men is shown by him who has trained himself by the discharge of the duties of marriage; by him, I say, who in the midst of his solicitude for his family shows himself inseparable from the love of God."[11]

Such sole mates are women or men who, through the duties and sacrifices of marriage, have trained themselves to love with God's love. They live out the gospel on a daily basis, forgiving, serving, and putting others first in the most ordinary issues of life (putting on a new roll of toilet paper instead of leaving a tiny shred, complimenting others for tasks instead of taking them for granted, being gracious instead of condemning when someone has had a hard day) in such a way that they see themselves as being in training to be godly (1 Timothy 4:7).

As Christ's follower — as a true sole mate — I'm called to take his example and his definition of love and apply it to my spouse. It really doesn't matter whether my spouse is a "soul mate," as much as it matters that I choose to love her with Christ's love. It means having a sacrificial mind-set marked by generosity, kindness, and mercy — for she certainly is my sole mate, my precious sister in Christ.

Become a biblical sole mate who walks in this truth, who daily travels God's journey of sacrificial love, and who willingly goes into training to be godly. This is a far more stable foundation on which to build a lifelong partnership than the theory of the philosopher Plato.

"Greater love has no one than this, that he lay down his life for his friends." It may not always be the most exciting love, but it is certainly the truest love.

16

Enjoying Each Other

I was on Jekyll Island, Georgia, speaking at a benefit for a pregnancy care center. The center put me up in a beautiful resort Jacuzzi room (alas, Lisa wasn't with me), right on the beach. I spent the bulk of my forty-eight hours there working, wanting to make full use of my time away from my family. But the afternoon of the benefit, God seemed to call me outside. The Lord and I went for a walk on the beach, and I had time to clear my thoughts and enjoy a quiet moment with him.

Sadly, I almost missed that walk. I love the ocean — it reminds me of how small I am, and the wind that invariably greets me I consider a welcome companion. But I felt so preoccupied with getting a lot done that, had it been up to me, I would have left Georgia without so much as touching a single grain of sand. God reminded me that, though work is important, he wants us to enjoy life, too.

The same principle holds true in marriage. We can become so consumed with the challenges of marriage — growing in character, doing the right thing, being a servant, getting all the tasks done, paying attention to our children (the list is endless) — that we forget to enjoy each other.

While I firmly believe growth in holiness is one of God's primary purposes behind marriage, it's not the only one. In fact, God's first stated reason for putting Eve with Adam was that "it is not good for the man to be alone" (Genesis 2:18). This points to companionship. And Deuteronomy 24:5 gave young men an entire year to focus on their wives' happiness: "If a man has recently married, he must not be sent to war or have any other duty laid on him. For one year he is to be free to stay at home and bring happiness to the wife he has married."

We give God glory when we learn to "enjoy the light" (Job 33:28). Accordingly, the Lord calls us into marriage so that we might enjoy each other. Please, let's not allow the realities of life — work, responsibilities, obligations, or even spiritual growth — to blind us to the necessity of enjoying each other's company.

You can't pick up a magazine without reading warnings that a couple shouldn't allow their sex life to wane — but why not just as many warnings that we shouldn't allow our enjoyment of each other to grow lukewarm? Certainly, sex can be part of this enjoyment, but I'm talking about the more common elements of appreciating each other. God could have decreed that I walk this earth by myself — but he has blessed me with a companion whose smile and occasionally giddy nature bring delight into many otherwise dreary days.

And yet our weeks and our evenings can get so busy that we miss times set aside for pure enjoyment. I used to laugh off "date nights" as impractical, but I've since come to see their essential place. A couple needs to set aside some regular time — and the "date" doesn't have to occur in the evening — when they get together simply to enjoy each other. This is God's good plan and design, his gracious gift to us.

When a couple tells me they've fallen into constant quarreling, nine times out of ten it's because their marriage has become utilitarian — who will pick up the kids, did you pay the bills, it's your turn to cook dinner tonight. And the element of enjoyment for pure pleasure goes sadly lacking.

When did you last take a step back and admire your spouse, thanking God you don't have to walk this life alone? When have you taken the time to enjoy a good conversation or a shared walk, or even watched a movie or read a book or went sailing together?

Jesus warned that some miracle workers can get so busy serving him that they cease to know him (Matthew 7:21–23). How utterly sad! In the same way, we can get so caught up in the "business" of marriage that we stop relating to, loving, and enjoying each other.

Some evening this week, why not shelve all the discussion about what needs to change, what needs to be done, who's at fault, who's going to drive the kids to soccer — and instead just go out and do what you like to do together? As you do so, recognize God as the author of this enjoyment. He designed us to enjoy each other, and we honor him when we experience this quiet pleasure.

"He redeemed my soul from going down to the pit, and I will live to enjoy the light."

17

Thoughtlessly Cruel

Remind the people to be ... peaceable and considerate, and to show true humility toward all men.

Titus 3:1–2

A couple of years ago, my wife planted blueberries beside our house, about seventy feet away from the nearest faucet. We had a cheap hose at the time that kept splitting as I hauled it across the lawn to water the blueberries. I had to cut the hose and reset a new nozzle every time it split, so I finally got fed up and went to the hardware store and got a "heavy-duty, industrial-strength" hose, *guaranteed* not to split.

I felt so happy with my purchase — finally, a decent hose! It made me smile, just looking at it. I'd pick it up, feel its weight, and say to myself, "No way this baby is *ever* gonna split."

Imagine my chagrin when Lisa barged into the house one evening and exclaimed, "I *hate* that stupid hose!"

My superindustrial-strength beauty proved far too heavy for my poor wife. When she tried to lug it across the front yard and the driveway to reach the side of our house, it felt like she was trying to pull a stubborn mule. I bought that hose thinking of me; I never even considered whether Lisa would be able to lift it.

Although some might consider this a simple inconsiderate act, at a deeper level it revealed my prideful self-centeredness. I didn't mean to act intentionally cruel, but I did act *thoughtlessly* cruel. I simply didn't pay attention to what was best for Lisa. Worse, I hadn't even thought about Lisa when I made the purchase. I had grown tired of repairing the hose, so I determined to make my own life better — as it turned out, at her expense. (We ultimately found a coiled hose that weighed much less but still stretched the necessary distance.)

Spiritual humility — what the ancients called "the queen of the virtues" — invites us to become more thoughtful, more aware, and more sensitive to others. In our arrogance, we can get so wrapped up in our own world that we can't see anyone else.

Humility is often built on the little things in life, and marriage is 90 percent small stuff. These small occurrences are, as writer Andrew Murray puts it, "the tests of eternity" because they reveal what's in our hearts.[12] We don't build humility on giant gestures as much as forge it with consistent, thoughtful actions, day after day.

This "queen of the virtues" so often gets misunderstood. We don't find humility by demeaning ourselves or criticizing ourselves or denying that God has given us obvious gifts and talents. Vertically, we find biblical humility by pointing others to the one true hero of Scripture, namely, God himself: "He must become greater; I must become less" (John 3:30). Horizontally, we find it by thinking less about ourselves and more about others (Philippians 2:4). We embrace humility when we refuse to get so wrapped up in our own worlds that we can examine what we are doing and saying in light of how our actions affect those around us. We find it when we stop pretending we are at the center of the universe, and instead adopt Jesus' attitude of becoming a servant of all (Mark 9:35) — which requires us to start *actively* thinking about others.

What better arena to learn this than in marriage? What relationship seems designed to confront our self-preoccupation more than living with a spouse?

In what areas in your marriage are you being thoughtlessly cruel? Where are you not even considering how your actions (or inactions) are making life difficult for your spouse?

Learn the joy of consideration. Free yourself from the constraints of being focused on yourself. Allow God to use your marriage to teach you to think of others.

18

You Deserve a Break Today

Remember the Sabbath day by keeping it holy.

Exodus 20:8

Sheila was married to a non-Christian for almost twenty-five years. Though initially she tried to pray fervently and every day for her husband's salvation, she eventually discovered that constant praying without a break was wearing her out. Through trial and error, Sheila found that she simply couldn't pray with equal fervor every day, but at various times, at the prompting of the Holy Spirit, she would enter renewed seasons of intercession — what she now calls her "seasons" of prayer. At the end of one such season, her husband became a believer — more than two decades after they had exchanged their wedding vows.

Sheila's "seasons" make sense to me. Very few spouses can pray intensely over one issue for twenty years. Marriage is a marathon, not a sprint, and at times we have to pace ourselves. That's why an "emotional Sabbath" can be your marriage's best friend.

A biblical view of marriage stresses the heart as a muscle more than as the center of emotion, and muscles need to rest and recover. When I returned to running after my fortieth birthday, I started reading up on modern training techniques. The biggest development over the past two decades seemed to be the crucial aspect of recovery time, as well as the idea of tapering before a long race. You work hard, and then you rest to give your muscles time to recover.

Relationships are no different.

If you're married to an unusually selfish or narcissistic person, a controlling person, a depressed spouse — or even if you're just wed to an average sinner — on some days you may say to yourself, "Today, I just need to survive."

That's OK. The idea of a Sabbath was God's, after all. If you truly are doing most of the giving in your marriage and rarely receiving, you may need to take a short breather — maybe you'll just go shopping, go out for a jog, watch a movie, or slip away for a long walk in the woods.

I'll admit, being married to Lisa, I have it easier than most. But even though I'm married to an agreeable person, on occasion the two of us will butt heads, which usually leads me to fret. My mind is sort of like a Crock-Pot — cooking up a slow-burning mess of stew. It's been a personal fault throughout my life.

On one occasion, I realized I needed, more than anything, just to turn my mind off. I went out by myself (many wives will hate me for suggesting this) and played eighteen holes of golf. Whenever a stray thought would come up, I forced myself to think about the tee shot, the approach shot, or the putt. I wasn't running from my problem — I was taking a break, so that I could look at the situation with fresh eyes and renewed energy.

There's a big difference between escape and refreshment. A genuine, biblical Sabbath of refreshment points back to work; we rest so that we can become even more engaged in the future. We take a break with a view toward returning to the task, asking God to refresh us in order that we might fulfill his high call to love our spouses. It's like sharpening the saw — we're doing something besides the direct work we're called to because in the end it will help us complete that work even better.

If you're in a difficult time in your marriage (and again, every marriage has such seasons), one of the best things you can do is to get out and laugh — find a few friends, rent a comedy, play with your kids, read a long novel, go on a men's or women's retreat. We are limited human beings with finite resources, yet the Bible calls us to a supernatural love beyond our strength. This should teach us two things: we need to radically depend on the Holy Spirit's empowerment, and we need to take breaks. Charles Spurgeon once said that many spiritual ills could be solved if we'd simply get a good night's sleep. Tiredness makes us resentful, bitter, petty, angry — and worse.

Good for you for being so conscientious about your marital responsibilities! God bless you for wanting to love your spouse like no one ever has and no one ever will. But remember — you're running a marathon. You can't keep sprinting. Sometimes you need true Sabbath rest.

Shaped by Sharing

Do not judge, or you too will be judged. For in the same way you judge others, you will be judged, and with the measure you use, it will be measured to you.

Matthew 7:1–2

In college, I had a pretty strict view about a "quiet time." I believed you were supposed to do certain things, and certain times of the day were better than others to do them in.

Then I started dating Lisa. Here was a woman who had a dynamic relationship with God but who rarely had a quiet time first thing in the morning. For starters, Lisa usually got out of bed just in time to make her first class. Not until later in the day would she go up on the roof of our dorm to lie in the sun during the afternoon. She brought her Bible along and called it a quiet time.

"At least be honest," I kidded her. "I mean, who goes up on the roof after lunch to pray and lay in the sun and calls that a quiet time?"

Then one day there was a loud knock on my dorm room door. I opened it up, Lisa marched in, and threw open my Bible to Acts 10:9: "About noon the following day . . . , Peter went up on the roof to pray."

Score one for Lisa.

Eventually, this insight — that different people pray in different ways — led to the writing of *Sacred Pathways*.

Fast-forward a few years. I sinned against Lisa deeply, hurting her about as much as I've ever hurt her — and probably as much as she's ever been hurt. Even so, Lisa stuck with me. I realized I had some enormous holes in my soul and some gaping tears in my spiritual fabric. After much prayer and study and repentance, the key truth of *Sacred Marriage* emerged. Though I didn't write the words for another decade, the groundwork for that book had been laid.

Many audiences have laughed about Lisa's and my different views of what constitutes food. Some of my college buddies still can't believe I can eat — and actually enjoy — a good tofu casserole, but I do every now and then. Lisa was one of the first people on the bandwagon of decrying the danger of trans fat, getting rid of everything in our house that included partially hydrogenated oil — and though I initially thought she was going off on another health food–magazine scare, it turned out she was right.

It stuns me to look back, in ways both profound (spiritual truth) and earthy (tofu versus Tator Tots casseroles), how much being married to Lisa for twenty years has changed me. We are who we are in part because of the persons we married. You've done what you've done in good measure as a couple. Sharing our lives shapes us.

Pause for a moment, and think about how living with your spouse has helped make you into the person you are. This is true even if your spouse isn't a believer. I've talked to many women who are married to some difficult men, and these wives have been astonished at the wisdom that sometimes slips out of their husbands' mouths, or at how God has used a particular issue to point out failings in their own lives. Yes, these women may have lacked spiritual intimacy, but they've learned to appreciate the strength, or the provision, or the loyalty of even an unbelieving man.

I think it's helpful to take a step back and let yourself be amazed at how God has used your wife or husband to help you become who you are. It's also essential for future growth. Once I recount how God has already used my spouse to help me grow, then I'll be more open to how he might continue using my spouse to help me grow in the present and the future. But one thing kills this learning process more than anything else: our tendency to judge our spouses rather than listen to them (and this may be especially true if your spouse isn't a believer, or if you perceive your spouse to be less spiritually mature than you are).

What strengths does your spouse possess that you lack and can learn from? Your spouse may be far from perfect; even so, what character quality does he or she have that you can admire and emulate? We're always so aware of the areas in which our spouses seem to be lacking; this week, concentrate on the strengths that can inspire you.

When I judged Lisa about her quiet time, I wasn't learning from her; I was building prejudice. When I faced challenges early on in our marriage, I blamed her instead of confronting my own sin and unrealistic expectations. When I ate what tasted good, regardless of what it contained, I was poisoning my body. I have been radically shaped, in matters both small and large, by sharing this life with Lisa.

I can't even imagine where or what I'd be if I hadn't asked Lisa to marry me. Although she's so different from me, and our strengths often come from opposite ends of the spectrum, God has used this curious mix to help both of us become what we are and accomplish what we have. Through the difficult and the easy, through the fun and the pain, through the encouragement and the repentance, God has shaped us — and he is shaping you as well.

Share — and be shaped!

I Hold You Responsible

Peter turned and saw that the disciple whom Jesus loved was following them.... When Peter saw him, he asked, "Lord, what about him?" Jesus answered, "If I want him to remain alive until I return, what is that to you? You must follow me."

John 21:20–23

One of my best friends is a marriage and family therapist. One summer, our families took a vacation together. When you do that, you see the good *and* the bad.

On one occasion, he saw the bad. He and I had been talking about a situation in my marriage in which I was struggling with an appropriate response. My friend knew this issue had been simmering in my relationship with Lisa for some time, but now he saw it firsthand.

"So you see what I'm trying to deal with?" I asked him.

"I do. But, buddy, I hold you responsible."

My friend then helped me see how a weakness of my own had exacerbated the situation. In fact, I think that's why this issue bugged me so much — it regularly pointed out to me where *I* was falling short, and I resented that.

We can't control how our spouses react, but we always remain responsible for how *we* react. One person's sin never excuses our own. In my case, I realized I was acting like a wimp. There's no more noble way to put it! I was so consumed with being a "nice" husband that I had become less than a good husband.

The next day I went on a long run, which is how I like to process things. I remember praying, "OK, God, we've established that I'm a wimp — but I don't know how to change. I've been like this my entire life. What should I do?"

Looking back, I'm amazed at how, just a day or two earlier, I had focused completely on what I thought Lisa was doing wrong and how Lisa needed to change. I felt sorry for myself and was more than a little frustrated. But my friend helped me see I could better spend my energies addressing the weakness that this situation was revealing in me.

Like Peter, I had insisted on saying, "Lord, what about *her*?" But just as Jesus challenged Peter, so he challenged me: "What is that to you? You must follow me." It was as if God was saying, "I'll deal with Lisa; right now, concern yourself with what *you* need to change."

I honestly believe just about every case of marital strife has this dynamic at work. God allows us to come together as two sinners, knowing we will be sinned against. Marriage is about learning how to respond to a sinful human being in a holy way. It's also about letting someone else's sin reveal our own.

Because we all marry sinners, I can't see any other way to look at it. None of us are married to perfect human beings. (The one perfect human — Jesus Christ — never married.) The reality of coping with someone else's sin never excuses us from fulfilling God's high call to keep on loving.

That's why Lisa and I have chosen to remain relatively transparent even to outsiders. I can't count the times someone has come up to us and said, "I just can't believe how transparent and vulnerable you and Lisa are in *Sacred Marriage*!" After hearing this a dozen or more times, Lisa and I went back and read through what I had written, worried that maybe we had been too vulnerable!

But after doing that, we still regretted nothing we said. We both acknowledge that we deal with sin every day, because we know that every couple deals with sin every day. It's time for all of us to acknowledge the reality of sin, and then to learn how to deal with it, rather than to pretend that some ugly realities don't exist, or that they can be solved in ten easy steps.

You may feel frustrated by an issue in your own marriage, and legitimately so. I know you're being sinned against, because I know you married a sinner. You're not the first in this situation, and you certainly won't be the last. Feeling sorry for yourself won't change anything. Changing spouses won't stop you from being sinned against either — all it will do is change the way you're sinned against!

One productive thing you *can* do is to take an honest look at how a character flaw of your own is contributing (notice, I didn't say "causing," which is too strong) to the situation, and ask God to help you overcome it. Seek godly counsel, listen to God in prayer, study what the Bible says about it. Use marital strife as a "mirror moment" that points out an area where God wants to change you.

Whenever you catch yourself saying, "Lord, what about him? What about her?" listen to Jesus responding, "What *about* them? *You* must follow me."

21

The Big Picture

But seek first his kingdom and his righteousness, and all these things will be given to you as well.

Matthew 6:33

Scene 1: While on a family vacation in Hawaii, Lisa was looking at me as if I had just lost my mind. We woke up very early that morning to go snorkeling, and everyone was feeling pretty tired by early afternoon. When I realized we had a few hours before we planned to be anywhere else, I announced that I intended to squeeze in a run.

"It's ninety degrees out!" Lisa exclaimed. "And the humidity is brutal. You want to kill yourself?" She couldn't understand why I wanted to pound the hot pavement instead of lie on the beach.

Scene 2: July 4th, back in Bellingham, Washington. Though I really love fireworks, I volunteered to stay home and do the dishes and watch our terrified dog while Lisa and the kids found a strategic place to view the city fireworks. As I lay next to our golden retriever (something that happens *only* on the Fourth of July), I heard the "grand finale," the cascade of explosions signifying the end of the show, and it dawned on me: I had just missed something I really enjoy seeing.

What was going on?

A greater dream fueled both scenarios. For a good bit of my adult life, I've harbored the dream of completing a marathon. Now that I'm in my forties (a fact my body reminds me of almost daily), I realized that if I didn't get this done soon, it would only become increasingly difficult. So I joined a local training group that prepared weekend athletes to run the Seattle Marathon. I followed their training schedule religiously — even in Hawaii.

I missed the fireworks because I had planned to do a group run early the next morning — July 5 — and I thought that if I stayed up late, I wouldn't be ready to do a hard training run.

Because I had the bigger picture in mind — finishing a marathon — the little sacrifices barely registered. The fact that the thermometer in Hawaii registered ninety degrees didn't carry as much weight as the fact that I needed to get in an hour run that day. The fact that I enjoy fireworks and would really miss them didn't even register until I heard, through the walls, what I was missing because I had been so focused on accomplishing this one goal.

If we ever lose the "bigger picture" in our marriages, we're headed for trouble. The big picture — glorifying God — will keep us from becoming consumed by the regular challenges marriage presents to our comfort. We become obsessed with not getting to do what we want to do or with our obligations, and soon, that's all we see. But when we keep the big picture in mind, we willingly endure the difficulties because the greater good — the future good — is even more important to us.

I can't tell you how many times I've reminded myself of one of the most important verses in the Bible: "But seek first his kingdom and his righteousness, and all these things will be given to you as well" (Matthew 6:33). When I strive to put God's kingdom first and focus on growing in his righteousness, it amazes me how quickly everything else falls into place.

Living in a marriage is sort of like putting together a jigsaw puzzle. You can become so myopic — just examining individual pieces — that occasionally you need to take a step back and look at the picture on the cover of the box to remind yourself exactly what you're trying to create. Likewise, we can become so fixated on the problems and challenges of marriage that we miss the ultimate purpose of every believer's life: seeking first — above all else — God's kingdom, and growing in righteousness and godly character.

A person who married solely for the sake of his or her marriage won't last if the marriage turns sour. If your primary purpose in being married is to be happily married, what will keep you in that marriage when your relationship becomes tough or distant or less than satisfying?

But when you decide to stay married to glorify God and to become more holy in his sight by remaining joyfully married to a sinner, you tend to view the smaller sacrifices as merely steps along the way to a much greater and glorious purpose. I didn't run in ninety-degree heat with high humidity because I considered it fun; I ran in sweltering weather because I wanted to complete a marathon several months later. I gave up watching fireworks in July because I had focused on what would happen in November — the Seattle Marathon. Author and educator Elton Trueblood once made this insightful observation:

> Family solidarity takes hard work, much imagination and constant self-criticism on the part of all the members of the sacred circle. A successful marriage is not one in which two people, beautifully matched, find each other and get along happily ever after because of this initial matching. It is, instead, a system by means of which persons who are sinful and contentious are so caught by a dream bigger than themselves that they work throughout the years, in spite of repeated disappointment, to make the dream come true.[13]

Don't get bogged down in the minutiae of marriage. Keep the bigger picture in mind. Such a view will carry us through the challenges marriage regularly brings our way.

If It's Not Sin . . .

Accept one another, then, just as Christ accepted you, in order to bring praise to God.

Romans 15:7

Wendy and Don joined eight other couples in their premarital class. During one session, everyone wrote down a list of their differences. Much to Don and Wendy's chagrin, their list ran longer than any other couple's — three full pages! "We were the one couple the counselors didn't think would survive," Wendy remembers, "but *we* knew we would."

After they got married, their personal differences started to become irritants. "I was always in a hurry," Wendy says, "and Don was so methodical. I flew by the seat of my pants, and he was so organized. I let things slide, but he had to know every little detail."

Inevitably, these personality differences created moments of tension — little frustrations that crept up at the grocery store, while sitting around at home, or as they carried out the basic rituals surrounding dinnertime. In the aftermath of one such moment, Wendy found herself praying, "God, what do you want me to do here? Show me what my response is supposed to be."

The tension had been building and now seemed about to boil over. Wendy felt "really frustrated and angry," but she had learned enough to ask God for his perspective on all of it. His insight sent Wendy to her knees. She felt suddenly overcome by peace, and God, in his gentle, quiet voice, whispered, "Wendy, if it's not sin, you can't demand that it change."

Wendy realized she could *ask* her husband to change, but she couldn't demand that he change or nag the change out of him. If the irritating action or character quality wasn't sin, she'd have to learn to put up with it — unless Don decided to change it voluntarily.

That quiet conversation with God radically changed Wendy's attitude toward her husband. "Just because Don is organized and methodical and meticulous and can take his time when I want him to hurry up, well, that's not sin," she said. "Yeah, it can be frustrating shopping with him sometimes, but I can't demand that he become like me. Accepting this really freed up our relationship, and I stopped being such a nag. After all, it was really *my* problem, not Don's. Once I accepted this, our marriage started to come together, and everything became easier. We still have our struggles and our moments, but when I hear others talk about their marriages, I think Don and I have an unusually good one."

In fact, though Wendy and Don were pegged as "least likely to succeed" out of the nine couples taking the premarital class, eighteen years later, they are the only couple still together.

God has used Wendy's insight to reach out to others as well. She works at a preschool, where a young mom confessed she was about to leave her husband.

"Why?" Wendy asked.

When the woman shared her reason, Wendy responded, "*All* men are like that. All you're going to do is leave a man who loves your kid to marry a different man who hates your kid, and eventually he'll do the same thing. Why in the world would you want to do that?"

Wendy later said she "feels horribly sad for men, because women don't understand them and fault them for not doing things they usually aren't equipped to do."

God's words to Wendy can revolutionize any marriage. The man or woman you're married to is his or her own person. Some things about him or her may not be to your liking, but if the things that bug you aren't sin, you have no right to demand that he or she change.

You may wish your husband would be more spontaneous or your wife less gregarious (or vice versa), but those are personality traits, not characteristics of sin.

If you persist in trying to change things that aren't sin issues, you're going to make your marriage life miserable. Dr. John Gottman, a leading marriage researcher, points out what he calls "one of the most surprising truths about marriage":

Most marital arguments cannot be resolved. Couples spend year after year trying to change each other's mind — but it can't be done. This is because most of their disagreements are rooted in fundamental differences of lifestyle, personality, or values. By fighting over these differences, all they succeed in doing is wasting their time and harming their marriage.[14]

If you've been working on an issue for ten years or more, and the issue is one of annoyance rather than morality, here's my how-to advice: Let it go. Repeat to yourself, "This will never change."

Instead of trying to resolve these differences, find harmony in accepting them and learning to live with them. Such a response calls us to humility, where we no longer assume that our way is the only way or even the best way.

Different people have different quirks. We married people with different backgrounds, different outlooks, and different personalities from ours. In fact, those very things often attracted us to our spouses in the first place. Even so, at times these backgrounds, outlooks, or personalities may frustrate us, anger us, or inconvenience us, but *if it's not sin, we can't demand change.*

"Accept one another, then, just as Christ accepted you, in order to bring praise to God" (Romans 15:7).

Greater Than the Sum of Their Parts

Two are better than one,
*   because they have a good return for their work:*
If one falls down,
*   his friend can help him up.*
But pity the man who falls
*   and has no one to help him up!*

Ecclesiastes 4:9–10

With a 30 handicap, Bob Andrews may sound like an average golfer.
    Until you learn that he's blind.
    Bob lost his eyesight during an attack while walking a Marine Corps patrol in Vietnam. Though he returned stateside stuck in a coma, his girlfriend, Tina, stayed by him. "I had to," she said. "My whole life was lying in that bed."[15]
    When Bob came out of the coma, he felt little excitement about life, wondering what a blind man could possibly do. Tina challenged Bob's unilateral thinking; if he were to think in team terms — he and Tina together — the limits would vanish. "Look," Tina assured him, "we're two people. We're a team. We can do anything we want!"
    Bob and Tina got married within two months of his return and immediately embarked on a life more active than most couples could imagine. Together, they have a business as building contractors. They have three sons, they sail, they fish, they bodysurf, and yes, they even golf. Tina lines up Bob, tells him how far to hit it, and Bob lets fly. When he putts, Bob reads the greens with his feet.
    After caddying for Bob one time, sportswriter Rick Reilly watched as Bob and Tina "sat next to each other like high school sweethearts. I half expected them to put two straws in his beer."

What's the secret to their happiness? Tom Sullivan, a blind actor and recording artist, gave Rick Reilly a clue:

> Every blind person is told at first that he's going to be dependent on others his whole life, and so they react wildly. They do anything they can to be independent. You know, walk into traffic, take up dangerous sports, stuff like that, stuff that will prove to the world that they don't need them. But it only makes them unhappier. Eventually, through love, they recognize that the only way to be happy and at peace is to live interdependently, to live knowing that they need others and others need them. And that's what blind golf is, a symbol of that lesson. The notion that we all need each other, blind or sighted.[16]

Rick's own reflections are equally touching: "I saw then what a team they had become — the broken soldier and the lost girlfriend. They were so much greater than the sum of their parts."

So many married couples resist this interdependence. They don't necessarily resent the person as much as they resent the relationship and its assumption of two people being shaped into one. They start doing selfish things to assert their independence, and they begin saying things like, "I can go do whatever I want! Why should I have to check with you?" "Who are you to tell me how I can spend my money?" "Look, you're not my mother [or father]. Get off my back!"

These and similar statements are cries for independence — but we gave that up the day we got married. We're part of a team now, and we have to think like a team. Maybe it's fear that makes you lash out like this; maybe it's pride, or maybe it's selfishness — whatever the cause, the effect is the same: disaster for the marriage.

You'll find true joy only in learning to work together and play together, and even in becoming dependent on each other. Burn your boats! Throw yourself recklessly into this marriage, as if there were no way out. That's the way to build interdependence and to experience the oneness the Bible describes as characterizing husband and wife. May this be said of every married couple: "They were so much more than the sum of their parts."

You're Prime!

Therefore encourage one another and build each other up.

1 Thessalonians 5:11

In the classic novel *Freckles* by Gene Stratton-Porter, a kindly couple gives a young man who is "intensely eager to belong somewhere" a new chance in life by offering him employment.[17] The boss's wife treats Freckles like a son, becoming the mother he never had. When Freckles's boss sees how this kindness leads the young boy to tears, he praises his wife:

> Sarah, you're a good woman, a mighty good woman. You have a way of speaking out at times that's like the inspired prophets of the Lord. . . . Did you see his face, woman? You sent him off looking like a white light of holiness had passed over and settled on him. You sent the lad off too happy for mortal words, Sarah. And you made me that proud of you! I wouldn't trade you and my share of the [forest] with any king you could mention.[18]

Pausing, the man looks straight into his wife's eyes and adds, "You're prime, Sarah, just prime!"

The same day my wife read that passage to our children on a long car ride, I had watched her come to the car and told her, "You know, you look *really* good today," and my wife responded with the typical wifely response: "You think so? Because my hair didn't quite turn out the way I had planned it, and I'm not sure about this shirt. It doesn't look quite right when I leave it out, but I'm not sure it works tucking it in, either, and — "

"Well," I added, cutting her off, "I think you look fantastic."

The Bible calls us to encourage each other, which is an active, ongoing obligation during times of challenge, stress, and even just everyday living. Consider how widely encouragement is urged and reported in Scripture:

- God to Moses: "Encourage [Joshua], because he will lead Israel" (Deuteronomy 1:38).
- Soldiers in the midst of battle: "The men of Israel encouraged one another" (Judges 20:22).
- Joab to Saul before a battle: "Now go out and encourage your men" (2 Samuel 19:7).
- Josiah to the priests: "[Josiah] appointed the priests to their duties and encouraged them in the service of the LORD's temple" (2 Chronicles 35:2).
- Paul and Silas to the early church: "After Paul and Silas came out of the prison, they went to Lydia's house, where they met with the brothers and encouraged them" (Acts 16:40).
- Paul to the disciples: "When the uproar had ended, Paul sent for the disciples and, after encouraging them, said good-by and set out for Macedonia" (Acts 20:1).

Consider a few general exhortations to encouragement:

- "But my mouth would encourage you; comfort from my lips would bring you relief" (Job 16:5).
- "Encourage the oppressed" (Isaiah 1:17).
- "Therefore encourage one another and build each other up, just as in fact you are doing" (1 Thessalonians 5:11).
- "But encourage one another daily, as long as it is called Today, so that none of you may be hardened by sin's deceitfulness" (Hebrews 3:13).
- "Let us encourage one another" (Hebrews 10:25).

Yet, in our selfish humanness, instead of thinking about encouraging, we may be tempted in our marriages to ask if *we're* being encouraged. In fact, I'll bet there are many wives who, after reading the quoted passage from *Freckles*, may even have thought, "Why doesn't my husband talk to me like that?" instead of asking, "Do I encourage my husband like that?" My friend Lisa Fetters observes that "women think we deserve this encouragement, and that men don't need it, but men *do* need to hear much encouragement."

When was the last time you looked in your lover's eyes and said (to use old-fashioned language), "You're prime, you know that?

You're really prime!'"? When was the last time you didn't take your spouse's hard work for granted — inside the home or outside it — and specifically thanked him or her for what he or she contributes to your life? Has it been so very long since you've put words to your thoughts and told your spouse specifically what you're feeling?

Don't measure yourself merely by what you *don't* do ("I don't come home drunk, I don't get into affairs, I don't waste our money"). Love is an *active* duty, and encouragement, as a biblical command, requires us to take the initiative. We live in a world that beats us down on an almost daily (if not hourly) basis. Marriage is designed as an oasis of encouragement, a way station where we can get renewed and refreshed with loyalty and kindness.

It's so easy to be complacently married, forgetting the need to unleash the active force of encouragement — but take this gentle reminder. Think of a few things, even now, and make sure another day doesn't go by before you look your spouse in the eye and say, "You're prime, just prime!"

Marital Ruts

See, I am doing a new thing!

Isaiah 43:19

One of the best things that happened to my marriage was breaking my wrist. The break was serious enough to require surgery, and suddenly, Lisa and I got thrust out of our routine. We did almost everything together, in part because I needed so much help. Since I had to limit my exercise to walking, we took near-daily strolls together. We shopped together. We answered email together (at first, I couldn't type). For a while, Lisa even helped me get dressed (OK, *you* try tying your shoe with one hand!).

Forced out of our routine, Lisa and I discovered a deeper and newer love. The romance was always there; it had just lain buried under layers of always doing the same thing. Isn't this really one of the greatest challenges many marriages face: the mind-numbing routine?

Theologian Paul Evdokimov insightfully fingers this reality in his classic work *The Sacrament of Love*: "The day-to-day profanes the sacred.... It is in the fearsome struggle against the duration and murderous repetitions that the human being appears most vulnerable. The prosaic in life brings him down to the infernal element of boredom."[19]

You don't have to break a wrist to rouse yourself from this boredom; sometimes just getting away will do the trick. Years later, Lisa and I spent a long weekend in New York City. Being together nonstop for five days suddenly made it seem strange the first time I left the house upon our return — something I had taken for granted so many times before. I got so used to having Lisa by my side — eating every meal with me, no kids asking us questions, no errands pulling us apart — that it seemed strange when we returned to the "real world." I noticed for several days afterward that I acted far more affectionate with Lisa — even better, I acted that way without even thinking about it.

Marriage is a long journey, and any long journey requires occasionally getting off the road to eat, to fill up the car with gas, or simply to rest. Has your love fallen into a rut? Is your marriage slowly getting buried under the daily routine? What can you do differently to break out of the box and renew your love for each other?

Maybe your rut is more behavioral — you've learned to tune out your spouse's voice, or you always make love in the same, predictable way or on the same, predictable night. Maybe you've completely stopped trying to find creative ways to demonstrate your affection and care. Perhaps you've become so ensconced in the workweek routine — the early-morning departure, the commute, the time away from home, coming back in the evening tired and grouchy — that you're completely missing opportunities to affirm and reconnect with each other.

Never underestimate the element of occasional surprise in delighting your spouse and building up your marriage. It can be so simple — a wife going to the trouble of picking out a book on tape that her husband can listen to on his morning commute; a husband buying his wife a completely unexpected gift, unconnected to any holiday or anniversary, for no other reason than to tell her he loves her. What would it mean to your spouse if you took an afternoon off — from work or watching the kids — to go to a matinee, take a walk around the lake, or go on a picnic? Sometimes all it takes is something out of the ordinary, something that says, "I don't take you — or us — for granted. I've put some special thought into this. I want to fight the 'murderous repetitions' and 'infernal element of boredom.'"

Through Ezekiel, God promised Israel, "I will give you a new heart and put a new spirit in you; I will remove from you your heart of stone and give you a heart of flesh" (Ezekiel 36:26). In the same way we can become calloused toward God, so we can become calloused toward each other. Pray for a new spirit and attitude toward your spouse, that your "heart of stone" will become a "heart of flesh."

Occasional ruts are inevitable in any long-term relationship, but they're never insurmountable. We can break out of them if we really want to.

26

To Make Her Holy

Just as Christ loved the church and gave himself up for her to make her holy.

Ephesians 5:25–26

When air travel resumed after the 9/11 terrorist attacks in the United States, commutes got a lot more difficult. Gone were the days when I could show up at our small regional airport thirty minutes before my flight. In fact, the airline I usually fly closed down all flights from Bellingham, meaning I now have to drive ninety miles to the Seattle airport.

To wait in lines.

To be asked to take off my shoes and walk in my socks through a metal detector.

To have a complete stranger open my suitcase, riffle through my underwear, and ask me what a particular medication is for (I'm not kidding). How I could possibly bring down or hijack an airplane with sinus medication ("Get back; I've got Tylenol, and I'm not afraid to use it!") is beyond me, but there you have it.

I grew irritable at the constant harassment. I just wanted to get through the airport, catch my flight, and reach my destination.

Several months later, Lisa was traveling with me to go to a conference — the first time we had flown together after the attacks. Lisa saw the brusque way I pushed through the airport, the lack of grace evident in my life as I muttered under my breath, and my overall demeanor — and she was appalled.

"Gary, would you just dial it back a bit? I've never seen you like this. What's the matter with you?"

I thought about what she said and realized she was right. I had become a practical atheist. I wasn't praying for people I saw. I wasn't looking for ministry opportunities. I was trying to survive — and doing so with a mean and critical spirit. Biblically, I believe a Christian without a mission is only half a Christian, but that's exactly what I had become — at least in the airport.

All that changed over the next several trips. Because Lisa had held up a mirror to my sin, I started praying for people I passed. I tried to be open to any opportunities where God might want to use me. And a certain joy entered my life, even while traveling.

I'm so thankful for this mirror God has given me in my wife. Please don't resent it when your spouse brings up an area that really *does* need to be addressed. We become blinded to our faults all too easily, and our spouses, who know us best, can lovingly point them out.

God calls believers to grow in righteousness: "You were taught, with regard to your former way of life, to put off your old self, which is being corrupted by its deceitful desires; to be made new in the attitude of your minds; and to put on the new self, created to be like God in true righteousness and holiness" (Ephesians 4:22–24). In the original Greek, the "putting off" is in the aorist tense — it is done once for all. But the "being made new" is in the present tense — it's an *ongoing* action. Marriage can feed this like nothing else.

In fact, Paul says that Christ loved the church by giving himself up for her "to make her holy" (Ephesians 5:26). If your spouse is a believer, she or he is your sister or brother in Christ; as fellow believers, we're called to encourage each other to grow in character. We express our love by being part of the ongoing process of renewal and growth in righteousness.

I'm so thankful that Lisa spoke up at the airport and continues to speak the truth in love. I'm grateful that her love for me is strong enough to confront me. I'd be a lesser man if I weren't married to her.

In her book *The Good Marriage*, psychologist Judith Wallerstein draws this wonderful conclusion:

A good marriage, I have come to understand, is transformative. The prevailing psychological view has been that the central dimensions of personality are fully established in childhood. But from my observations, men and women come to adulthood unfinished, and over the course of a marriage they change each other profoundly. The very act of living closely together for a long time brings about inner change, not just conscious accommodation.... As the men and women in good marriages respond to their partners' emotional and sexual needs and wishes, they grow and influence each other. The needs of one's partner and children become as important as one's own needs. Ways of thinking, self-image, self-esteem, and values all have the potential for change.[20]

Marriage is a mirror. At times, we may not like what we see, but if we resolve not to shy away from the reflection — or worse, crack the mirror — it can be a very valuable spiritual tool.

27

Marriage Is Movement

Behold, I am coming soon!

Revelation 22:12

Lisa and I went to see the movie *Seabiscuit* with Rob and Jill, two of our closest friends. At the start of the movie, I sat by Rob and Lisa sat by Jill, so that Lisa and Jill could share the unbuttered popcorn and Rob and I could assault our arteries with the buttered kind. But halfway through the movie, Lisa had to get up for a moment, and Rob slipped over to sit by his wife.

There was something wonderfully refreshing in seeing a man who has been married for eighteen years still eager to sit by his wife for the last hour of a movie. That simple movement said a great deal about Rob and Jill's marriage, and it personifies a biblical truth.

I heard of one wedding in which the *bridegroom* actually walked down the aisle instead of the bride, in order to capture the biblical picture of Christ — *the* bridegroom — going to his bride, the church. As Christ pursues the church, so the husband is to pursue his wife. (Note to future husbands: it's the rare woman indeed who would even *consider* giving up that famous walk down the aisle; I wouldn't recommend trying this at home!)

Marriage is more than a commitment; it is a movement toward someone. Husbands, are you still moving toward your wife? Or have you settled in, assuming you know her as well as she can be known, and thus turning your sights to other discoveries and challenges? Even worse, are you violating your vows with the "silent treatment" or a refusal to communicate?

Wives, are you moving toward your husband? Are you still pursuing him, seeking to get to know him, trying to draw closer to him? Have you considered new ways to please and pleasure him, or have you become stagnant in judgment, falling back to see if he'll come after *you*?

Jesus moves toward us even in our sin; will we move toward our spouses even in theirs?

Movement is about more than communication; it's about the force of our wills. Are we choosing to pursue greater intimacy in our relationship? Do we seek to resolve conflict, or do we push it aside, assuming it's "not worth the hassle" while letting our love grow colder? Are we still trying to understand our spouses' worlds — their temptations and trials, their frustrations and challenges — or are we too consumed with our own? Are we praying for our spouses, encouraging them to grow in grace and holiness, or are we tearing them down behind their backs, gossiping about them so that everyone will feel sorry for how difficult we have it?

Honestly ask yourself, "Do I know my spouse any better today than I did three years ago?" If not, maybe you've stopped moving toward your spouse. And if you've stopped moving toward your spouse, you've stopped being married in the fully biblical sense of the word.

This week, why not launch yourself on a new exploration — your spouse? Why not see what new things you can learn — how you can grow even closer to each other, how you can give up a little more independence and embrace a little more interdependence? Why not make a renewed attempt to study your spouse every bit as much as a biology student studies the movement of cells under a microscope or a seminary student pores over thick reference books late into the night?

So many people say the "excitement" has left their marriage. Well, exploration is one of the most exciting journeys known to humankind. Most of the globe has been mapped, many times over — but that person who wears your ring? There are still secrets yet unknown and yet to be explored on that side of the bed.

Get busy.

28

Earthly Education
for Heavenly Heights

And now these three remain: faith, hope and love. But the greatest of these is love.

1 Corinthians 13:13

Henry Drummond (1851–1897) wrote a remarkable little classic titled *The Greatest Thing in the World* in which he points out that when Paul defines love in his letter to the Corinthians, he's referring to how we treat people. This emphasis on loving other people, Drummond believes, is a thread throughout the New Testament: "We hear much of love to God; Christ spoke much of love to man."[21]

Drummond argues that if love is the greatest thing, then it should be the primary pursuit of our lives:

> The supreme work to which we need to address ourselves in this world [is] to learn Love. Is life not full of opportunities for learning Love? Every man and woman every day has a thousand of them. The world is not a playground; it is a schoolroom. Life is not a holiday, but an education. And the one eternal lesson for us all is *how better we can love.*[22]

Marriage is a primary place where people learn this — through lots of practice. People improve in athletics through practice; we improve in music, writing, and cooking through practice. We practice in order to overcome our failure and inadequacies. Drummond stresses the importance of practice:

> If a man does not exercise his arm, he develops no biceps muscle; and if a man does not exercise his soul, he acquires no muscle in his soul, no strength of character, no vigor of moral fiber, nor beauty of spiritual growth. Love is not a thing of

enthusiastic emotion. It is a rich, strong, manly, vigorous expression of the whole round Christian character — the Christ-like nature in its fullest development. And the constituents of this great character are only to be built up by ceaseless practice.[23]

This is so good I have to repeat it: the love we seek is not "a thing of enthusiastic emotion" but rather a Christlike character "built up by ceaseless practice." Thus, marriage is about learning to adopt "the greatest thing in the world" by practicing our ability to love while living with a sinner.

In the first flush of infatuation, lovelike activity comes spontaneously. It gushes out of us. We say nice things, we buy presents, we write encouragements, we are eager and creative lovers, we do all the things that make someone feel special. Why? Because "enthusiastic emotion" moves us to do so. But if we stop loving when the feelings fade, we reveal that we are motivated by mere emotions more than by God's call on our lives, that we pay more attention to feelings than to Christ's glorious invitation to love as he loved.

If we dodge this character-producing practice by running to divorce court or by pouting and withdrawing into silent marriages, our hearts start to calcify spiritually. Our hearts shrink instead of enlarge, and we reinforce the selfishness that already screams for pride of place. But if we *practice* loving — even when we don't feel like it — our hearts bulge with God's goodness and generosity until love becomes the natural expression and response to God's work in our lives.

That's why infatuation doesn't really teach us to love. Only marriage can do that. Infatuation comes naturally — it is innate, no practice required. But a marriage is built on the bedrock of many considered decisions: Will I love, or will I hold a grudge? Will I serve, or will I be selfish? Will I notice this person, or will I retreat into my own world? Will I please my spouse, or will I draw pleasure from ignoring him [or her]? Marriage reveals and then purifies our motivations in a way that infatuation never can.

In fact, if our hearts are right and if we truly desire to become like Christ, we won't resent the challenges of marriage but will welcome them instead. Drummond gives this sound advice:

Do not quarrel ... with your lot in life. Do not complain of its never-ceasing cares, its petty environment, the vexations you have to stand, the small and sordid souls you have to live and work with. . . . That is the practice which God appoints you; and it is having its work in making you patient, and humble, and generous, and unselfish, and kind, and courteous. Do not grudge the hand that is molding the still too shapeless image within you. It is growing more beautiful though you see it not, and every touch of temptation may add to its perfection. Therefore keep in the midst of life [and marriage!]. Do not isolate yourself. Be among men, and among things, and among troubles, and difficulties, and obstacles.[24]

Certain elements of the Christian faith must be developed in solitude. The traditional disciplines of fasting, prayer, study, and meditation are necessary building blocks — but Christian character requires *community*. Marriage can give us this community, and more. It can usher us into the greatest thing in the world — by providing us, every day, the practice field on which we can learn how to love. The mundane and often routine duties of life provide an earthly education that can take us to heavenly heights.

One

We who are strong ought to bear with the failings of the weak and not to please ourselves. Each of us should please his neighbor for his good, to build him up. For even Christ did not please himself.

Romans 15:1–3

Lisa and I were talking with a counselor about one of our children, who can be greatly affected by tension. In talking with the counselor, this child identified me as the laid-back one, while admitting that Lisa can occasionally get tense. I'm ashamed and embarrassed to admit that part of me expected the counselor to really let Lisa have it, but in a stroke of genius, the counselor turned to me and said, "So, anything you can do, Gary, to release the pressure off Lisa would be really helpful."

Like Jesus, she dropped the responsibility right back into my own lap.

Too many times in marriage we forget we're one. We start operating as individuals, even occasionally setting ourselves up against each other, forgetting that God is making us into a single unit. We may not go so far as to have a financial prenuptial agreement (which mocks the marriage before it even begins), but we carry an *emotional* prenuptial agreement — looking out for ourselves at the expense of the union.

If you sense your spouse lacks something, rather than criticize or judge him or her, your job is to pick up the extra load. I hear many wives complain that their husbands aren't as spiritually mature as they are; they use this fact as a club to make their husbands feel guilty and inferior. But Paul says we should do the opposite: "We who are strong ought to bear with the failings of the weak and not to please ourselves. Each of us should please his neighbor for his good, *to build him up.* For even Christ did not please himself" (Romans 15:1–3, italics added).

If we're so "strong," then our calling is to bear with the "weak." Now, it's never the case that one person is always strong in everything while the other spouse is always weak in everything. At times Lisa feels frustrated that I'm *too* laid-back and not forceful enough. Lisa and a counselor would have many opportunities to pick apart my own faults if we discussed other issues in our family. But rather than point fingers, we're called by God to fill in the cracks.

Marriage as an institution is a stroke of genius on God's part. As sinful humans, all of us lack certain skills, and all of us enter this relationship with myriad limitations and faults. By joining two individuals, God creates a much stronger unit on which he can build a family. It truly is a wondrous work: two individuals coming together to fill in where the other lacks. But this dynamic will take place only when we stop using our spouses' shortcomings as ammunition and instead use them as a call to step up. United in God, we are one.

If you were at a ball game and the batter hit a foul ball that was headed straight for your nose, your arm wouldn't sit back and say to itself, "It's about time the nose got what was coming to it. That nose gets so much attention, while I just hang here on the side of the body. I hope that ball really hurts!" On the contrary, without even thinking, you'd raise your arm to cover your face. You'd do it instinctively, even if your arm was broken and in a cast. Why? Your body acts like a single unit.

Marriage thrives spiritually when we die to our singleness and are resurrected to a divine union. We are to support our spouses in all they lack, and they are to support us in the same way. And if you're tempted to say, "But my spouse doesn't watch my back, so why should I watch his [or hers]?!" go back and read the first three verses of Romans 15 one more time: "We who are strong ought to bear with the failings of the weak and not to please ourselves. Each of us should please his neighbor for his good, to build him up. For even Christ did not please himself."

The day you exchanged vows, you promised to join your finances, your future, your family, your welfare — everything you have — with this one other person. It's a waste of spiritual energy to obsess over a spouse's fault; instead, we're called to figure out what we can do to make this sacred relationship work.

30

The Happiness
That Follows Holiness

Remembering the words the Lord Jesus himself said: "It is more blessed to give than to receive."

Acts 20:35

On radio programs, at seminars, and in churches across the country, I'm often asked what I mean by the subtitle of my book *Sacred Marriage*: "What if God designed marriage to make us holy more than to make us happy?"

Please note, I didn't write *"instead of* to make us happy" — Christians, of course, seek happiness like everyone else. The difference is the *means* by which we pursue happiness, and what we find our happiness *in*. Holiness and true happiness are not adversaries; they are allies. They do not go to war with each other but rather build each other up. This is not to say, however, that they are equals. Biblical happiness is the offspring of holiness, giving holiness the pride of place as the parent.

Henry Drummond, whom we met on pages 97–99, writes, "There is only one thing greater than happiness in the world, and that is holiness; and it is not in our keeping; but what God has put in our power is the happiness of those about us, and that is largely to be secured by our being kind to them."[25]

What a profound thought! We can't fully determine how others treat us, but we can determine how we treat others — and God has made us in such a way that how we treat others in the little routines of life lays the foundation for our own happiness.

I fear, though, that the contemporary meaning of *happy* doesn't do justice to either Scripture or Drummond. Perhaps *joy* is a better choice for modern readers, as I've heard many people say, "Doesn't

God want me to be happy?" as justification for leaving their spouses and taking up with someone else. In today's society, "happy" has been reduced to "euphoria."

Drummond takes us deeper, telling us to find our happiness not in an emotional response but in a sacrificial policy called love:

> Where Love is, God is. He that dwelleth in Love dwelleth in God. God is love. Therefore *love*. Without distinction, without calculation, without procrastination, love.... Lose no chance of giving pleasure. For that is the ceaseless and anonymous triumph of a truly loving spirit. I will pass through this world but once. Any good thing therefore that I can do, or any kindness that I can show to any human being, let me do it now. Let me not defer it or neglect it, for I shall not pass this way again.[26]

Can anyone doubt that such an attitude would refresh, reenergize, and revolutionize virtually every marriage on the face of this earth? If each spouse would honestly say, "Any kindness I can do to my spouse, any act of affection, any motion of goodwill, let me do it now. I don't know how long I have left to live, so let me not defer or neglect any act of kindness, but let me truly *love*."

Each of us can choose to do this individually, regardless of how our spouses respond. Their actions toward us are not in our keeping, but our ability to be kind and giving lies entirely within our realm. And the beauty of God's creation is that when we love, we experience God—and that's what brings true happiness. When we act in love, we invite God into our house, and God brings a soul-fulfilling joy that transcends contemporary notions of mere euphoria.

When marriages break down, they often do so in a context of resentment and a feeling that we're not getting what we need or want. But looked at in the light of love, this enemy loses all its power and place: "The most obvious lesson in Christ's teaching," Drummond writes, "is that there is no happiness in having and getting anything, but only in giving. I repeat, *There is no happiness in having, or in getting, but only in giving*. And half the world is on the wrong scent in the pursuit of happiness. They think it consists in having and getting, and in being served by others. It consists in giving and serving others.... He that would be happy, let him remember that there is but one way—it is more blessed, it is more happy, to give than to receive."[27]

Great minds think alike. Albert Schweitzer once told a group of graduating seniors, "I don't know what your destiny will be, but one thing I know: the only ones among you who will be really happy are those who have sought and found how to serve."

Do you seek happiness? Then seek to love. Move toward your spouse. Serve him. Love her. Cherish him. Sacrifice for her. Don't miss a single opportunity to demonstrate a kindness or to speak some word of affirmation. In doing so, you will invite God into your life, home, and soul, and you will find true biblical happiness.

31

Running from Yourself

For by the grace given me I say to every one of you: Do not think of yourself more highly than you ought, but rather think of yourself with sober judgment.

Romans 12:3

Ever wonder why Hollywood romances rarely last even thirty-six months? I have a theory.

Our culture virtually worships actors. They receive constant adulation, praise, and admiration, and they know they are the objects of many fantasies. But marriage unleashes reality. Within a real relationship, a spouse discovers that an actor smells just like the rest of us. They can be just as petty, just as selfish, just as demeaning, and just as despicable (sometimes even more so).

One time, after a nearly sleepless night in a hotel, tossing and turning all night long, I finally glanced in the mirror and was shocked at what I saw: the tired eyes, the messed-up hair, the pale color. I said to myself, "Gary, at this moment you may well be the ugliest person on the face of this planet."

Looking at our reflection through the mirror of our marriage can be equally hard to take. We feel horrified by how we've acted — astonished by our own selfishness, pettiness, laziness, or even cruelty. Satan can use this awareness to tempt us to run. In truth, we don't want to run just from our spouses; we also want to run from ourselves, the persons we were in our marriages. We want to be with someone new who hasn't seen our bad side. Some may even try to deceive themselves into thinking their spouses were at fault for bringing out the flaws in them. We think we can just start over, and the bad side won't follow.

This, of course, is the great myth. We have enough energy either to run from who we are, or to cooperate with God's Holy Spirit in changing who we are, but we never have enough to do both. It will always be one or the other.

Actors who love to receive praise may have a particularly difficult time coping with someone who looks at them with unjaundiced eyes. What must it feel like to be shown larger than life on fifty-foot screens, then to go home and see a look of absolute disdain on the face of your spouse? To have photographers beg you to stop for a picture after you've spent hours fixing your hair, getting into your clothes, and creating that look, then to go home and take off the makeup, sleep on the hair, and wake up in a T-shirt instead of a tuxedo or a Vera Wang dress?

This is slightly more than a theory — I read the words of a top Hollywood actor who said, "Here's the great thing about dating. You get to start over and go, 'I'm a really nice guy.'" He freely admitted he wasn't a consistently "nice guy" in his earlier relationships, but dating someone new gave him a chance to start over — until the real man acted out once again.

But the permanence of marriage forces us to admit we haven't been as nice to our spouses as we wish we had been. It encourages us to evaluate ourselves with, in Paul's words, "sober judgment." Some painful memories will tempt us to run. Some snapshots will make us wince and cause us to think, "I wasn't a really nice guy; I was a *horrible* guy."

But if we accept that God designed marriage to help us grow in holiness, we know, going in, that we're a work in progress. Instead of running from these hurtful revelations, we can welcome them, realizing that our marriage is showing us what we need to know and pointing out where we need to grow.

Rather than run from ourselves, we can focus on *changing* ourselves! Let's be honest — some things about you and me are ugly. If we marry, our spouses will see that ugliness, whether it's an attitude, a habit, a disposition — whatever. After marriage does its work and this weakness gets exposed, we'll have a decision to make: Will we run from this revelation into the arms of another person who doesn't yet know our weakness, or will we embrace the call to grow in holiness, accepting Scripture's admonition to "think of [ourselves] with sober judgment"?

Don't run from yourself. Be humble, stay where you are, and focus on changing your attitudes and actions instead of your spouse.

32

Good in Bed

Thus I have become in his eyes
like one bringing contentment.

Song of Songs 8:10

"Don't let this lawyerly facade fool you," Sandra Bullock warned Hugh Grant in the movie *Two Weeks' Notice*. "I'm actually really good in bed."

I was eating an airline dinner, flying somewhere over the Midwest, when I put on the headphones and caught this piece of dialogue. In a Christian worldview, a single person wouldn't know whether he or she was "good in bed." But since I was stuck in an aluminum tube 30,000 feet above the ground, I had plenty of time to think, and the question challenged me in another context.

When did I last ask myself whether *I* was good in bed? While it's a grave mistake to reduce sex to mere mechanics, the question can go much deeper: When did I last *care* about that question? And why do so many women's magazines that cater to singles feature this question, while publications reaching out to married couples almost never even raise it?

How sad, I thought, that a single woman who has no long-term interest in a man could be more determined to please her boyfriend sexually than a married woman would be in pleasing her husband. Shame on me if I spend less time thinking about how to pleasure my wife than a single man might think about how to keep his girlfriend interested!

We have to fight against taking our spouses — and our responsibilities — for granted. And taking them for granted is easy to do, because on the day we marry, we gain a monopoly of sorts. Our spouses commit to have sexual relations with no one else. In a faithful marriage there exists no competition or even comparison. The only intimate life our spouses can and will enjoy is the intimate life we choose to give them. Regardless of whether we act thoughtfully, creatively, or selfishly in bed, they receive *only* what we provide. It's sheer laziness if I give less attention and care to the mother of my children than some twenty-something kid gives to a young woman he met mere weeks ago.

Rather than make us careless, this exclusivity should make us grateful, and therefore even more eager to please our mates. The principle goes well beyond the bedroom, of course. You're the primary person for intimate talk and encouragement. Are you "good in communication" too? You're the first person who should be supporting your spouse in prayer. Are you "good in prayer"?

But let's not act as though the bedroom is unimportant: When did you last ask yourself, "Am I endeavoring to please my spouse in bed?" If we're slacking in this area, our spouses can't really do much about it — but *we* can, and we should.

Here are some questions to ask: Do I want to reward my wife's commitment to me, or do I want to make her regret it? Do I want to bless her, or will I take her for granted? Do I want to be a generous lover, or am I content to be a miser who reluctantly doles out occasional "favors"? Am I creative? Am I enthusiastic? Am I initiating?

Honestly ask yourself, "Am I good in bed?"

33

Divine Detachment

For without [God], who can ... find enjoyment?

Ecclesiastes 2:25

I'm convinced one of God's purposes for marriage is to create a divine disillusionment. He needs to bring us to the end of our belief that anyone other than God can ever fully satisfy us. I've talked to countless couples whose problems remain throughout the years — often discussed, yet never resolved. In such cases, a sense of betrayal almost always comes to the surface: "He won't do what I *need* him to do," or, "She just won't do what I *want* her to do."

When the desires are legitimate (better communication, more support, more sexual availability), the pain of denial is keenly felt; but demands — even legitimate ones — still represent the Achilles' heel of every person's contentment. Spiritually, demands place us at the mercy of sinful persons who are limited in their ability to love. If we look to anyone other than God to meet our deepest needs, we are guaranteeing frustration.

You might feel frustrated because of far too little action in the bedroom — but what will you say to the couple who wrote to me after the husband had an industrial accident, a pair now facing a future without *ever* experiencing sexual intercourse again? Should the wife be free to pursue someone else sexually?

Of course not.

She has a legitimate desire for sexual intercourse — but it must remain unfulfilled.

You may well feel frustrated that your husband doesn't support you emotionally the way you'd like him to — but what about the wife whose husband gets kidnapped on the mission field and who doesn't even hear from him for two full years?

She has a legitimate desire for support, a listening ear, an aptly spoken word — but it can't come from her husband.

Any desire can be obstructed and thereby bring frustration. We do not have an absolute right to anything. Rather, we have an obligation to trust that God, in his providence, will ultimately provide what we need — or will give us strength to do without.

I can already hear many of you arguing the point. The Christian virtue of detachment — which means we stop finding our meaning and security in people, things, position, money, and power and instead focus our needs on God — scores little popularity in today's culture, but it remains as true today as when the ancients touted it and Jesus taught it.[28]

In fact, I'll go out on a limb and claim it's somewhat healthy to feel a little disillusioned in your marriage, because it's at that point you'll realize you need to look to God for your highest joy. You may feel tempted to respond to disillusionment by searching for another spouse who promises to "fulfill" you more, but eventually you would find that, while she had strengths your spouse lacked, she was missing some of your spouse's better qualities. Life with that new person would inevitably bring its own disillusionment, until one day you'd wake up to the fact that your soul's happiness really does depend on a holy, perfect God — not a sinful human being.

John 15:13 says that Jesus, on the cross, demonstrated the greatest love ever known — laying down his life for his friends — but for every movie made about that kind of sacrificial act of love, thousands more extol romantic love. The fact is, our culture idolizes romantic love and looks teary-eyed at the meeting of "soul mates," and it yawns at Christ's work on the cross. May God save us from this idolatry! As wonderful as romantic love may be, it should never compete in my heart with Jesus' work of redemption where my deepest needs were fully met. Any other love — including every kind ever portrayed by Tom Cruise or Julia Roberts — is a far lesser love; it's an inferior love, the value of which assumes meaning only because of Jesus' preeminent love.

So your spouse has disappointed and continues to disappoint you? Thank God. You're in a great place. You're in the doorway of detachment, where you can learn to let go of the expectations of the created and fall into the arms of the Creator. Our Lord took the same journey. Jesus "detached" himself from heaven to come to earth. He left his earthly parents to assume his ministry as the Messiah. He died to currying favor with the crowds so that he could become the crowd's Savior. He even detached himself from spiritually experiencing his Father's presence so that he could bear our sin. And then he willingly detached himself from life on earth so that he could die for our sins.

Would you be like this Savior? Then die to your demands. Be resurrected to utter dependence on your heavenly Father, who has loved you, is loving you, and will always love you like no one else can, including your spouse.

Make Someone Happy

A happy heart makes the face cheerful,
but heartache crushes the spirit.

Proverbs 15:13

A cruel and abusive father towered over the childhood of Pat Conroy, author of *The Great Santini* and other popular novels. Pat's earliest memory is sitting in a high chair, watching his mother go at his father with a knife, while his father laughed and knocked her away.

Pat went on to attend a military college, where in his plebe year he suffered malicious attacks, degradation, pain, and embarrassment. During this difficult time, Pat got to know a married couple, who provided him with an island of sanity in an otherwise chaotic and hostile world. Pat recounts that during one visit, he felt transfixed by the healthy and adoring attitude the husband and wife expressed toward each other, something he had never witnessed at home. He wrote, "It made me happy to see how much she loved him."[29]

It made me happy to see how much she loved him.

While so many couples obsess about whether their spouses are making *them* happy, many of us don't realize how we can make *others* happy by loving our spouses well. We can't control whether our spouses act in a way that brings us happiness, but we can control how we love — and how we love can bring great happiness to others.

For starters, loving his daughter or son well will certainly bring happiness to the God who created him or her. In the same way that my children's future spouses can make me happy by being generous with their love and tolerant toward my kids' faults, so God delights in watching how I treat my wife — his daughter.

We also make our children happy when we treat each other with affection and kindness. I remember one time, while on a walk with my wife, Lisa and I held hands and laughed. Our oldest daughter came up behind us and said, "You two are so cute!" Seeing us love each other put a smile in her heart.

Loving our spouses well will certainly bring happiness to our in-laws, to our pastors, to our community, to young couples desperately searching for hope in their own marriages and thus eagerly on the lookout for role models, and to many others who watch us without our even knowing about it. People love it when they see adoring love, generous love, kind love, and committed love displayed in this jaded, fallen world.

I remember watching the Academy Awards as an Oscar-winning actor paid tribute to his wife during his acceptance speech. I know exactly where this man stands on virtually every political issue, in large part because our views are so radically different that I can pretty much assume we'll be on the opposite side of any debate. From the public comments he's made, I doubt we'll ever vote for the same candidate for president (or even dogcatcher). Yet when I saw him acknowledge his wife — genuine tears filling his eyes, and true, sincere affection in hers — I felt surprisingly moved. This couple's outspoken political activism may make me nauseous, but their love makes me smile.

This phenomenon — making others happy by our love — has remained true throughout the centuries. Almost three thousand years ago Homer wrote, "There is nothing nobler or more admirable than when two people who see eye to eye keep house as man and wife, confounding their enemies and delighting their friends."

Make someone happy today — by loving your spouse. You may not realize who is watching, but I'll guarantee you this: someone is.

I Love Him Anyway

"If you love those who love you, what credit is that to you? Even 'sinners' love those who love them. And if you do good to those who are good to you, what credit is that to you? Even 'sinners' do that. And if you lend to those from whom you expect repayment, what credit is that to you? Even 'sinners' lend to 'sinners,' expecting to be repaid in full. But love your enemies, do good to them, and lend to them without expecting to get anything back. Then your reward will be great, and you will be sons of the Most High, because he is kind to the ungrateful and wicked. Be merciful, just as your Father is merciful."

Luke 6:32–36

Meg and Peter have been married for more than twenty years. On Valentine's Day, Meg went all out, giving Peter his favorite candy, tickets to an upcoming hockey game, and later at night, she wrapped herself in a special outfit purchased for just that occasion.

Peter got her a card.

At the grocery store.

That he purchased on the way home from work.

He didn't add anything to it either. He just signed it: "Peter." He even forgot to write the word "Love."

A couple of days later, Meg tried to explain that she felt a little taken for granted. Apparently, Peter misunderstood her intent because when, two months later, they celebrated their twenty-second anniversary, Peter didn't get Meg *anything*.

Meg waited throughout the day, wondering when Peter would bring out the present — but the present never came. Since she had given Peter *her* present — some rather expensive fishing lures — she knew Peter had to know it was their anniversary. So as they got ready for bed, Meg waited in anticipation, but Peter slipped in beside her and promptly went to sleep.

The next morning, Meg was beside herself. She fretted all day until Peter came home from work, and then she asked, "How could you not get me anything for our anniversary — especially after our conversation about Valentine's Day?"

"Well, I thought about getting you something, but it didn't work out," he replied. "And I knew not to get you a card because you said you didn't like it last time."

"It's not that I didn't like the card. It's just that the card alone seemed a little *sparse*. But even that's better than nothing."

Several months later, Meg had a birthday. This time, Peter got her a present — a kitchen tool set. Several weeks before, Meg had asked to borrow Peter's tape measure and screwdriver. Peter figured Meg should have her own small set of kitchen tools so she didn't have to borrow his.

Meg recounted all this, then explained how she had tried to get her husband to read several how-to books on loving your spouse, but it just didn't interest him. He'd read the first few pages, lose interest, and never pick up the book again.

"I've realized it's never going to change," she confessed. "But I love him anyway."

That last statement — "But I love him anyway" — is one of the most profound theological statements on marriage I've ever heard. Most of us base love on "because," not on "anyway." I love you "because" you're good to me. I'll love you "because" you're kind, because you're considerate, because you keep the romance alive.

But in Luke 6:32–36, Jesus says we shouldn't love "because"; we should love "anyway." If we love someone because he's good to us, or she gives back to us, or he's kind to us, we're acting no better than your average, everyday, common sinner who lives without the regenerating influence of the Holy Spirit. In essence, Jesus is saying, "You don't need the Holy Spirit to love a man who remembers every anniversary — not just the anniversary of your marriage but the anniversary of your first date and your first kiss — or who even remembers what you were wearing the first time you saw each other. Any woman could love a man like that. And if you love a husband who is kind and good to you — who lavishes you with gifts, who reciprocates with back rubs, who goes out of his way to get you time off from around-the-house duties, and who is physically affectionate even when he doesn't want sex in return — well, you're doing what any woman would do. There's no special credit in that!

"But if you love a man who disappoints you, who may forget an anniversary or two, who can be a little selfish or a little self-absorbed — now you're loving 'anyway,' and that's what I call my followers to do. In doing that, you're following the model of the heavenly Father, who loves the ungrateful and the wicked."

Will you love only "because"? Or are you willing to love "anyway"? Will you love a man or woman who doesn't appreciate your sacrifice on his or her behalf? Will you love a husband or wife who takes you for granted? Will you love a spouse who isn't nearly as kind to you as you are to him or her?

If your answer is "No," then at least admit this: You're acting just like someone who has never known the Lord. Almost every faithless marriage is based on "because" love. Christians are called to "anyway" love. That's what makes us different. That's what gives glory to God. That's what helps us appreciate God's love for us, because God loves *us* "anyway." He loved us when we rebelled against him. He keeps loving us when we continue to sin against him. He gives and gives — and we take him for granted, the height of ungratefulness. He is eager to meet with us, and we get too busy to slow down and notice him. He is good to us, and we accuse him mercilessly when every little thing doesn't go just the way we planned it; in other words, we can be wicked.

But God loves us anyway. To love anyway is to love like God and to learn about God's love for us, who loves the "ungrateful and wicked."

That's love, Jesus style.

Let's love like that.

A Spiritually Tight Marriage

Let love and faithfulness never leave you;
bind them around your neck,
write them on the tablet of your heart.

Proverbs 3:3

Have you ever paused to consider the almost heroic vulnerability we assume when we get married? We pledge to be sexually and spiritually faithful to a person whose body can easily succumb to disease, accident, and corruption — and the Bible doesn't offer sexual prenuptial clauses! If your wife were to have a medical accident and end up in a coma and on a feeding tube, you would still be obligated, out of reverence for God, to remain absolutely faithful to her. No leering glances at other women. No pornography. No inappropriate relationships with any other female. Your Christian obligation would call you to remain true to your wife until the day she died. Like some of the couples who have written to me, you might well be facing the possibility of *never again* experiencing sexual intercourse — but still, your Christian duty calls you to remain completely and utterly faithful. That's the commitment you made on the day you entered Christian marriage and promised your wife that, as long as both of you live, she will be the only, the sole, the exclusive, object of your sexual desire.

You might think a Christian wife, recognizing how vulnerable her husband has made himself on her behalf, would feel beside herself with gratitude. You might think, from a spiritual perspective, she'd go out of her way to be a generous and grateful lover. If she really understood the risks this man was taking on her behalf, you might imagine she'd naturally respond by becoming an extravagant and enthusiastic lover.

But why is this so often not the case? Why, in fact, is it usually the exception? The answer: We don't have spiritually "tight" marriages.

Most men, even Christian men, don't truly make themselves this vulnerable. They opt for a conditional faithfulness, like the French count who responded to the question, "Are you faithful to your wife?" with a droll, "Frequently." If their wives cooperate in the bedroom, then they'll remain mentally faithful. But if their wives cool down, ignore them, get too busy, or the men themselves just get bored or restless while traveling on business or away with their buddies, then they make exceptions and allow themselves to look, to fantasize, to take sexual pleasure (either directly through an affair or indirectly through the eyes or mind) from another woman.

Women, spiritually intuitive as they are, know this. And the marriage enters a gray wasteland. The husband is neither faithful nor vulnerable, so the wife feels no gratitude. Together, they never experience the true heights of sexual fidelity and faithfulness.

It's no coincidence that the stereotypical sin for men is to become voyeurs, while for women it's to become exhibitionists. Both sins assault God's perfect plan for the exclusivity of marriage. Though God calls a man to focus all his sexual attention on one woman, he decides to seek sexual satisfaction from women in general. He looks wherever he wants to look. Sometimes he even touches whomever he wants to touch. He has spent his entire life seeking satisfaction from the female gender instead of waiting and then setting his desire on one female in particular. This makes him less inclined to move toward one particular woman, and it rips apart the exclusive foundation on which an intimate marriage is based.

In the same way, a woman gets tempted away from biblical modesty to seek approval from men in general. Instead of finding her sense of fulfillment in pleasing one man, a wife may dress in such a way that she knows excites sexual interest from men in general. Receiving this attention — and perhaps even comparing it to the lack of attention she gets from her husband — a woman feels less concerned about her husband's connection to her. As long as she feels appreciated, she doesn't need any particular man's affection. Once again, the intimate wall has been breached.

The man is not faithful, the woman is not grateful, and they never experience a spiritually healthy sex life.

Consider this analogy. If I snack all afternoon long, when I come to the dinner table, I'm not going to eat with relish or with thankfulness. I'll nibble — if it tastes good. I'll notice it — if it's special. But I won't feel hungry. I won't truly *desire* that meal. And it won't cross my mind to express gratitude that my wife has gone to the trouble to prepare it. My wife will sense this meal isn't really important to me. Over time, she'll learn that she wastes her efforts in trying to make it special, so the quality of the meals plunges. Eventually, she may understandably ask, "What's the use?" and throw a TV dinner my way — and I may have become so used to snacking that, in one sense, I hardly even notice and, worse, really don't care. I'll just be thinking about the snacking I can do later.

How sad — but that's the truth in many a marital bedroom.

What's the way out? Become more absolute. Become more extreme. Keep the marital circle completely tight.

Listen: God designed marriage based on *need*: Adam needed a helper (Genesis 2:18). God also said that Eve's desire would be for her husband (Genesis 3:16). The language is so explicit here that one commentator calls it a spiritual desire "bordering on disease."[30] Voyeurism and exhibitionism destroy the psychological and spiritual basis of pure desire. A diluted focus creates a diluted desire. Husbands and wives who nibble all day long stop needing each other. Not needing each other, they show no particular gratitude when sexual desires are met — because the marital bed becomes just one place among many where sexual desires get fulfilled.

Repentance is the first step on the way back to Eden. Men need to remain absolutely, utterly, and completely faithful. A man should focus 100 percent of his sexual desire on his wife. He should recognize that she is the only appropriate person on whom he should lavish his mental, physical, and spiritual affection.

In return, a woman should dress in public as Paul tells her to dress — attractively but modestly ("I also want women to dress modestly, with decency and propriety" [1 Timothy 2:9]). In private, however, a wife should take great pleasure in arousing her husband's interest. She should revel in that power — God gave it to her! She should delight in the hold she has over this man. She should be generous and grateful that he would make himself so completely vulnerable on her behalf. And she should be eager to reward his exclusivity, for as long as it is in her power to do so (as he should eagerly reward hers).

Spiritually, a woman will find it far more fulfilling to be exclusively desired, adored, enjoyed, and practically worshiped by one man than she ever will from eliciting leering, lascivious looks from men in general. Why? Because that's the way God made us.

God's call is certainly extreme! One man experiencing sexual relations with just one woman — for an entire life. No sex before marriage. No sex with anyone else during marriage. Not even thoughts of sex with someone else. If, for any reason, sex as a couple becomes impossible, each partner remains obligated to maintain the exclusive sexual relationship.

While this sounds extreme and absurd to a lust-riddled society, I'd put the sexual satisfaction of a couple who lived their life this way against that of someone with wandering eyes or immodest appearance any day of the week. A couple focused on each other experiences something other couples never do: a satisfaction that touches the depths of the soul. God knows how he made us; his instructions for how we should relate are based on knowledge the world denies. We are not evolutionary accidents for whom the sexual urge is merely a naturalistic response. We are intricate spiritual beings, created for God's pleasure and designed to give each other pleasure. This design goes far beyond physical nerve endings to include the spiritual and emotional reality of being created in the image of God. Therefore, in the more transcendent part of our souls, we value fidelity, belonging, and holiness over the mechanical eruption of an orgasm. Not that we disdain orgasms. Far from it! But we recognize the appropriate place for sexual climax. Outside its proper context, "the act" loses its spiritual beauty, its emotional meaning, and its ultimate purpose.

Keep the marriage "tight." Become extreme. Throw yourselves at each other while becoming blind, sexually, to everyone else. Only then will you know God's full design and intentions for true sexual satisfaction.

37

The Great Escape

Do not fret because of evil men
or be envious of those who do wrong....
Trust in the LORD and do good;
dwell in the land and enjoy safe pasture.

Psalm 37:1, 3

Frank has been a drug addict for a dozen years. He is currently going through Narcotics Anonymous. Mary works for a boss who gets wicked pleasure from making his employees miserable. Richard pastors a church in which a rogue elder is doing his level best to wrestle leaders for control of the congregation.

All three of these people have something wonderful in common: They have access to God's great escape — marriage.

I don't know about you, but I have a tendency to fret. I stew over problems. I bring the anxieties and concerns home, and they hang like a low-lying cloud over my head, covering my demeanor and affecting my spirit.

But here's the wonderful, soul-scouring truth of marriage: It gives us something else to focus on. Fretters know it's hard to stop thinking about any particular concern unless you can focus on something else; marriage gives us that something else.

Take Frank, for example. He and I talked about how drug addiction tends to make people even more self-centered than they normally are. Even recovery can become "all about me" as they look for people to support them and as they focus on getting through the day without resorting to drugs. But holiness must strike sin at its root, and since one of the roots of sin is selfishness, Frank needed to find something to make it *not* about him — perhaps for the first time in his adult life.

That "something" was actually "someone" — his wife. "Every day," I said to him, "you've been waking up asking, 'How can I get those drugs?' or, 'How can I cover my tracks?' and more recently, 'How can I make it through this day?' But now, you have the opportunity to use your marriage as a way to focus on someone else. Wake up every morning and ask God, 'Lord, how can I love my wife today like she's never been or ever will be loved?' You've said yourself that you've made her life miserable for over a decade. Now's your chance to spoil her. Think about her when you're tempted to think about drugs or to dwell on yourself. Do all you can to love her and serve her and affirm her. Lose yourself in adoring her, and experience the joy — perhaps for the first time in your life — of selfless living."

Mary had an inviting opportunity because of her experiences with her tyrannical boss. Like me, Mary is a big-time fretter. As she went to bed each night, she had a hard time fighting back the bitterness and resentment aroused by her boss's venom and malice. If she woke up in the middle of the night, she could forget about going back to sleep; invariably, her mind fixated on her boss's latest fiasco, and she found herself silently fighting him all night long.

"Instead of thinking about your boss's ego," I told Mary, "think about your husband's strengths. Tell him why you respect him. Write notes that express why you admire him. Turn every temptation regarding getting back at your boss into an invitation to love your spouse. Eventually, Satan will get the hint, but even if he doesn't, your husband is going to feel really special! Either way, you win."

Richard's opportunity came as a result of his struggle with the power-hungry elder. For many pastors, the church can become an extension of who they are — a mistress of sorts. Now Richard has the opportunity to place the matter in God's hands while making sure that his heart remains fully invested at home. As a pastor, he needs to respond to this elder's shenanigans — but he shouldn't fret because of this evil man. How not to fret? Every time he feels tempted to think about the rogue elder, he can instead focus on doing something special for his wife. He can love her, just as Christ loves the church. If Richard does this faithfully, this elder may be one of the best things that ever happened to Richard's marriage.

What about your situation? How can God use as a great escape your call to love one person like he or she has never been or ever will be loved? What spiritual travail do you face that you can overcome by turning all the negative thinking and fretting into a positive act of love and affirmation?

One of the great blessings of marriage is that the call to love is so pervasive, so comprehensive, so time-consuming, and so gigantic that it really does provide a great and healthy escape from a world in which evil people dwell. If, like me, you have a difficult time keeping yourself from fretting, stop resisting and start substituting. Use every temptation to fret as a call to pray for, and act lovingly toward, your spouse. This week, revel in God's great escape.

38

Sanctuary

Your love is more delightful than wine.... Your name is like perfume poured out.

Song of Songs 1:2, 3

Nancy Belcher and her husband, Chris, arrived in Italy to run the Venice Marathon. They registered in a town called Mestre which, like many Italian cities, doesn't allow cars in the city center. Nancy told Chris she'd jog to the registration area, pick up their packets, and meet him back outside after he found a place to park.

But after Nancy picked up the race packets and left to look for her husband, she found herself surrounded by six thousand runners and their family members, most of them drinking, laughing, and talking in different languages. Nancy spent a frantic hour looking for Chris; they hadn't planned a meeting place, nor did they yet have a hotel room. They intended to just meet and then check in somewhere, but everything felt so new and so disorienting that Nancy had no clue where to look for Chris — and it was all so crowded!

Finally, Nancy remembered Chris had a cell phone, so with the help of an Italian desk clerk, she called her husband. Initially, Nancy felt reassured to hear the dial tone, but her heart sank when she heard a ringing in her purse — she had Chris's cell phone!

It was now 9:30 p.m., the night before the marathon, and as Nancy noted, "I had no dinner, no car, no hotel, and no husband."[31]

Nancy wandered back into the registration area, milling around aimlessly until finally she heard her husband's familiar whistle. At that moment, it was the most beautiful sound she could imagine: "I felt so relieved I hugged him and started to cry. My reaction so surprised him that he started to laugh. There we stood, among thousands of partying marathoners in an unfamiliar foreign city, crying and laughing."

I love this story because it's a picture of the sanctuary that marriage can become. In a foreign land, the one familiar face Nancy wanted to see more than any other was that of her husband, Chris. We may walk in a crazy world, but if we're married, we have the privilege, the refuge, the sense of security, the sense of comfort, pictured in Nancy and Chris's embrace.

Of course, we don't have to leave home to appreciate this sanctuary. A man with whom I hadn't had a significant conversation in more than ten years once publicly attacked me. Though the charges later proved silly, it certainly felt sobering to become the focus of such venom. One night during this ordeal my wife snuggled up to me, kissed the back of my neck, and said, "I love you, Gary." Earlier in the day, she had told me how a woman had apologized to her because when they first met, the woman had said, "Oh, you're Gary Thomas's wife! I heard him on Focus on the Family." The woman said she was sorry she had defined Lisa by her spouse, but Lisa told her, "You don't have to apologize. I love being known as Gary's wife!"

When you're attacked, it does something wonderful to your soul when your spouse glories in your relationship. Lisa knows me better than anyone else. She knows more of my history, more of my temptations, and more of my private devotion than any other human. She has spent more time with me, shared more words with me, and eaten more meals with me than anyone else.

Even so, she loves me. In fact, she even loves being known as my wife!

Her affirmation in the midst of such an ordeal, the reality of being deeply loved by the person who knows me best, provided a wonderful sanctuary where I could find shelter.

A few weeks later, the roles got reversed. A woman who didn't understand Lisa's situation misread her motives and erroneously applied a Bible verse to back up her rather blunt opinion. Lisa cried as we talked on the phone. "Honey," I said, "I know you better than that woman ever will. She doesn't understand your situation, and furthermore, biblically, she's just wrong. You're doing the right thing."

"You really think so?" Lisa asked.

"I *know* so."

There is great leverage when the person who knows you best can encourage you most.

In a good number of these devotions, I've talked about some of the struggles of marriage — how it's worth the pain, how it calls us to sacrifice, commitment, and so forth — but please, let's not forget the great joy and blessing of being known and being loved. Our marriages can become sanctuaries, sheltering us from a world that hates us. We might be lost in a foreign country, attacked in our hometown, challenged in our own Bible study, but what a joy to find refuge in the arms of a loving spouse!

The Bible is honest — evil people exist:

- "The wicked plot against the righteous and gnash their teeth at them" (Psalm 37:12).
- "And pray that we may be delivered from wicked and evil men, for not everyone has faith" (2 Thessalonians 3:2).
- Jesus said, "Blessed are you when [note: not *if*, but *when*] people insult you, persecute you and falsely say all kinds of evil against you because of me" (Matthew 5:11).

There are those who will tear us down, assume we have evil motivations, be inclined to think the worst of us, and even misrepresent us to others. They will gossip, slander, and ridicule. But God has given us a mate, a shelter in the storm, who knows us better than anyone.

When that mate loves us, adores us, and respects us, what it does to our souls is without question one of the most gratifying experiences in all of human existence. It is a powerful, powerful ministry to honor and adore your spouse, to become his or her sanctuary in a world that often seems predisposed to hate, to wound, to hurt, and to tear down.

Because you know your spouse better than anyone else, you have the opportunity to minister to him or her on a much deeper level. When Lisa said she loved me at just the time I needed it most, when she made a point of telling me how delighted she is to be known as my wife, she won my loyalty for life. She already had it, of course. It's what I had promised on the day we got married. But in those words, uttered when I needed them most, she unleashed a new torrent of thanks and affection to accompany that original commitment.

Lisa and I have faced our share of trials and troubles — but I would cross this world on Lisa's behalf. I would face all the demons in hell to defend her. She has been my sanctuary — and I will adore her for all of eternity.

Real People

Light is sweet,
and it pleases the eyes to see the sun.
However many years a man may live,
let him enjoy them all.
But let him remember the days of darkness,
for they will be many.

Ecclesiastes 11:7–8

I was speaking at a "Sacred Marriage" seminar at a hotel about two hours away from the host church. On Saturday night I spoke on sexual intimacy, and afterward the leaders handed out candles and Hershey's Kisses for the couples' private evening together.

This has happened several times before. Given the situation (at a hotel far from home, away from the kids), the setup (a Saturday night talk on sex), the intimate gifts (a candle, and on one occasion, massage oil and bath salts), the conversation that inevitably follows ("Well, honey, I guess we better go apply the Word!"), everybody all but knows that practically everybody else is going to enjoy sexual intimacy that night. The seminar host even made a point of saying the Sunday morning session wouldn't start until 10:00 a.m., "so you can sleep in" (wink, wink).

While Lisa wasn't with me, I did have the fun of watching Clemson beat up on Florida State in a college football contest — not quite as satisfying as sex, of course, but as I pointed out to some of the attendees, my entertainment lasted a good bit longer than theirs did!

I also had a chance to pray, and I came back the next morning with a word of comfort, as I guessed that at least one and perhaps several couples felt frustrated that, for whatever reason, they didn't enjoy sexual intimacy — and therefore felt even worse about their marriage than they had before. They knew what their friends were doing, and they may have felt cheated about their own circumstances. I stressed that it is unwise to evaluate your marriage based on any given moment. Marriage is a long journey, with many seasons; that reality, plus the fact that we are married to real people, with real physical and emotional problems, can combine to create frustrating moments. In such times, I said, we need to die to our expectations and focus on our obligations — loving them "anyway."

That night I got to apply my own words. Because I had spoken to two groups back to back, I had been gone almost an entire week, and I was *really* missing Lisa — in more ways than one! Unfortunately, her period arrived two hours before I did.

That kind of thing doesn't happen in the movies, or in novels, or in the latest Top 40 song.

But it's real life.

Lisa was so apologetic. Later that evening as I put the kids to bed, she got out of the bathtub and said, "I'm supposed to be doing all this and you're supposed to be resting and — "

I cut her off. "I'm just glad to be home," I said.

I'm married to a real person. In real life, marriage moments don't always turn out the way we wish they would. That's why I think we have to guard against expectations that deny our fallen condition in a fallen world. Sickness, frustration, the frailty and foibles of the human body, eventually find their way into most homes. If we don't expect this, then we make an already difficult situation that much worse, acting as though we're the only couple facing such struggles when, in fact, virtually every couple faces a variety of similar issues. It may not be at the same time we do (that's where comparisons become dishonest), but eventually, all marriages face most of the same hurdles. Eagerly anticipated moments collapse into agonizing disappointments.

That's why I believe we have to exchange our expectations for our obligations. Instead of focusing on what I *wish* would happen, I should concentrate on my duty and call to love. In this fallen world, there are many things we simply can't control. If we place ourselves at the mercy of these things, we become spiritual slaves, easily frustrated and discouraged.

But when I live by my obligations to love and to serve and to remain faithful, I rise above the circumstances of this fallen world.

Whatever happens, my duty is clear, and my marriage — my *real* marriage to a *real* person — is served.

Expectations assault a marriage that doesn't live up to perfection; obligations protect a marriage at its weakest moments. Expectations slowly wear down a marriage, while fulfilling obligations steadily builds up that union. Expectations foster fear and disappointment; meeting our obligations births intimacy and love.

In most cases, expectations are the enemy, and obligations are the protector. By which one are you going to live your life?

40

A Difficult Road

"I tell you that anyone who divorces his wife, except for marital
unfaithfulness, and marries another woman commits adultery." The
disciples said to him, "If this is the situation between a husband and
wife, it is better not to marry." Jesus replied, "Not everyone can accept
this word, but only those to whom it has been given.... The one who
can accept this should accept it."

Matthew 19:9–12

Some how-to marriage books fall short by presuming that the difficulties of marriage can be overcome. Every marriage, no matter how you look at it, is hard and will be hard.

That's why I like to correct a spouse who says, "I have a difficult marriage." There's no need to personalize it: "*I* have a difficult marriage." At various points, *every* marriage is difficult. The problem isn't necessarily with *your* marriage, it's with marriage in general.

Let's look at the honesty of the ancients who went before us. I'm not necessarily endorsing all of the following comments, but it helps to get a historical perspective on how earlier generations viewed marriage.

When Jesus told his disciples that marriage was for life and that only adultery could break its bonds, they immediately blurted out, "If this is the situation between a husband and wife, it is better not to marry" (Matthew 19:9).

Jesus doesn't refute this! He simply says, "The one who can accept this should accept it."

Chrysostom, a fourth-century church father, argues that when Paul attacks divorce, his real aim is to dissuade people from getting married: "For anyone who hears that, after marriage, he will no longer be his own but will be subject to the will of his wife ... will not even take the yoke upon himself, since once he has done so, he must be a slave as long as it pleases his wife."[32]

Cicero says this: "Is a man free when he is under a woman's orders? She imposes laws, prescribes, commands, forbids whatever seems good to her; and as for refusing when she gives a command, he cannot or dare not. In my opinion he should be called, not a slave but the most wretched of slaves, though he be born of the noblest family."

A writer from the Council of Trent has a word for prospective wives:

> Subject to her husband in everything, she must put up with his moodiness, contrariness, nights of eating too much and drinking too much, jealousy, suspicions, incontinence, adulteries, quarrels, blows. She must follow him, be with him everywhere, obey and serve him like a slave. . . . He uses up the money they have on dice, card games, drink, dinners, lavish gifts, ruinous contracts, ill-advised lawsuits and other ways, and the wife can apply no remedy.

And Jerome, writing in the fourth century, gives this whimsical warning to prospective husbands:

> Then throughout entire nights [you must endure] the long-winded complaints: "That woman has nicer things to wear outside. . . . Why were you looking at the woman next door? . . . What did you bring back with you from the forum?" No friend may we have, no companion. She suspects that love of the others is hatred for her. Then, too, there is no chance to try a wife out. You take her as she is. If she is hot-tempered, lazy, deformed, conceited, ugly — whatever defect there is, you learn after the wedding. . . . You have to keep noticing her face all the time and praising her and telling her how pretty she is for fear that, if you look at another woman, she'll think she's unattractive. If you entrust the entire house to her to be managed, you have to be her servant. If you reserve anything to your own judgment, she doesn't think you trust her. Then she turns to hatred and quarrels; and if you don't look out at once, she'll get some poison ready.

Jacques-Bénigne Bossuet, a French preacher from the late 1600s, made this observation:

Each [spouse] has moods, prejudices, habits, associations. Whatever be the things they have in common, people's dispositions are always different enough to cause a frequent chafing in so long a life together. They see each other so near at hand, so often, with so many defects on either side, in the most natural situations and ones so unexpected that it is impossible to be prepared. They get tired. The thrill is gone. The other's imperfection is irritating. Human nature makes itself felt more and more.... They love their cross, I am happy to say, but what they are carrying *is* the cross.

Even the patient and pastoral Fénelon warned, "They get tired of each other in this need of being almost always together and acting in unison on every occasion. It requires a great grace and great fidelity to the grace received to bear this yoke patiently.... A person must prepare for it in a spirit of penance when he believes he is called to it by God."

In an ironic way, I hope this honesty encourages you. When you grow discouraged, when you ask, "Am I the only one who struggles like this?" when you wonder why, at times, the requirements of marriage seem so burdensome, take heart in knowing you are not alone. You've chosen a difficult life.

But if marriage is so hard, why stick with it? For starters, except for those called to celibacy, marriage is God's will for us. It's how he designed us to live. But secondly, there can be great glory in tackling an almost impossible challenge. Marriage is based on a grand design created by God, extremely difficult but in some peculiar way extraordinarily satisfying. How else can we explain why two people who describe their marriage as "hell on earth" get divorced and then both get remarried within twenty-four months? Even knowing how painful it can be, they can't wait to jump back in and give it another try, albeit with someone else.

It's not so much that *your* marriage is difficult; the *state* of marriage is difficult. Don't be discouraged. It's the price we pay for a glorious return. Certainly, there's a place for the how-to approach; we *can* learn how to communicate better, how to resolve conflict, and a

host of other skills. But we *can't* overcome the reality that it'll nev
be easy to be married.

I originally wanted to title my book *Sacred Marriage* something
else: *The Greatest Challenge in the World*. I know of few other challenges
like it; certainly, I can't imagine any that last as long and test you so
personally and so deeply. But that, in an odd sort of way, is its very
appeal: "The one who can accept this should accept it."

The difficulty of marriage is both its challenge and its glory. It
can make us, and it can break us. It may indeed be a difficult road,
but it is a holy road that can lead us toward God.

The Ministry of Noticing

O LORD, you have searched me
and you know me.
You know when I sit and when I rise;
you perceive my thoughts from afar.
You discern my going out and my lying down;
you are familiar with all my ways.

Psalm 139:1–3

It started off as your average marriage morning. Lisa and I went out for an early walk, then stopped off at a Starbucks on our way to the grocery store to get some items for dinner later in the day. As Lisa walked up the steps, she turned and looked at me to say something. I remember the way the morning sun highlighted her hair, and I thought, "She is so beautiful to me."

Ten minutes later, I told Lisa what I had been thinking. "This has been a rather mundane marriage morning — going for a walk, getting a cup of coffee, stopping at a grocery store — but I just want you to know, when you paused on the steps I thought to myself, 'I am deliriously in love with that woman.'"

"Buuuuttt — ," Lisa said.

"No 'but.' That's it."

"That's it?"

"That's it."

"Oooh, baby, what do you want?"

"I don't want anything! I was just thinking I'm still deliriously in love with you after almost twenty years of marriage and thought I should share it with you."

"No, I mean it. You name it, you've got it."

For the voyeuristically curious, I kissed her on the forehead and left the room (not that it's any of your business!), struck by the power of simply *noticing* my wife and telling her about it. It dawned on me that this is what much of God's love is all about. He notices us. He doesn't take us for granted. The rest of the world is usually too busy to pay attention, but God remains passionately interested in and meticulously aware of our situation in life.

There was a time when Israel amounted to nothing but a tiny, insignificant family. But God noticed them: "The LORD did not set his affection on you and choose you because you were more numerous than other peoples, for you were the fewest of all peoples" (Deuteronomy 7:7). Even so, God chose this "fewest of all peoples" to become his "treasured possession" (7:6).

While on earth, Jesus carried on this same ministry. He noticed those whom the Pharisees in their religious blindness had forgotten. He paid attention to the woman at the well, a woman other "respectable" rabbis would have ignored. He welcomed children into his circle instead of shooing them away. He put up with repentant prostitutes and focused his ministry on those who seemingly could offer the least to his work: "Go back and report to John what you hear and see: The blind receive sight, the lame walk, those who have leprosy are cured, the deaf hear, the dead are raised, and the good news is preached to the poor" (Matthew 11:5).

So when Paul tells husbands we're supposed to love our wives like Christ loves the church (Ephesians 5:25), for one thing, he's telling us we're supposed to *notice* them. Everyone else may take them for granted, but not us. Their bosses or employees, their children, maybe even their parents, may be too busy to slow down and offer much by way of gratitude or encouragement, but it's our job to take the time to notice and affirm them.

Wives, you can do this as well. Particularly by the time we reach middle age and our bodies soften while our hair thins (or disappears), and younger men get promoted over us while youthful dreams die — when we feel invisible to the rest of the world — you can replenish our souls by not taking us for granted, by simply noticing your husbands and telling them what you're thinking.

Some of my most intimate moments with my heavenly Father come when I realize he's watching, he's noticing, he's getting it all down. When I pray, he sees. When I give, he takes notice. When I overcome a temptation that no one else knows about, he encourages me. He knows "when I sit and when I rise," he "perceives my thoughts from afar." He knows when I go out and when I lie down. He is "familiar with all my ways." Where can I flee from his Spirit? Nowhere. Where can I hide from his presence? That place doesn't exist (Psalm 139:1–10).

Loving begins with noticing. It is more than that, surely, but it can never be *less* than that. I argue in *Sacred Marriage* that the opposite of love isn't hate; it's apathy. Apathy is a form of blindness, becoming oblivious to another person. If I want to truly love my spouse, I must begin by remaining aware of her, noticing her, and letting her know all the while what I'm thinking.

We live in a self-absorbed world where we are all taken for granted in one form or another. May God grant us the grace to notice our spouses and love them like God loves us.

Notice your spouse this week — and then *tell him* what you're noticing.

One Day at a Time

And God is able to make all grace abound to you, so that in all things at all times, having all that you need, you will abound in every good work.

2 Corinthians 9:8

The spiritual brilliance of marriage can also seem like its greatest curse. Because God has created a relationship that only death is to break, we have the security of working through issues we might otherwise feel tempted to run from. But that blessing can, during difficult seasons, seem like a curse. Because only death or adultery can break the bonds of marriage, it may sometimes feel like the dark season we're in has no end in sight — night without a coming dawn, winter with no ensuing spring.

And that can make us panic.

It all comes down to how we look at it. When I ran my first marathon, I had a clear goal in mind. Because the usual mistake is to go out too fast, I made an ironclad decision to run the first thirteen miles at a certain pace. When I started to feel the strain, I didn't think, "How can I keep this up for another two hours?" Instead, I told myself, "Just focus on this: can you run the next mile in this amount of time?" Taking it one mile at a time, I ran the race much faster than my goal pace.

If you're in a difficult season in your marriage and you start to think, "How can I take another ten or twenty or, God forbid, thirty years of this?" you're headed for trouble. You're asking God to give you the grace for something that hasn't happened. Instead, break it down to a single unit — a single day: "Just focus on this: can I love my husband [or wife] for this day?" Don't think about ten years down the road, or even ten months! Can you love your spouse *for this one day*?

Some friends who knew I was running the Seattle Marathon asked me, "How did you do that for twenty-six miles?"

My answer? "One mile at a time."

How do you stay married for twenty-six years?

One day at a time.

Break it down. Focus on the here and now. Put the future in God's hands. Some miles will seem easy, and some will feel hard, but you need to focus only on the one you're currently running. Let the others remain in his care.

Can you love your spouse *for this one day*?

You Don't Understand: Role Reversals

Lisa accompanied me on a trip out East when everything started going wrong. Our flight out of Seattle got delayed, we had to stand in line for forty-five minutes to get our rental car, meals had to be put off, and so on. Our heads didn't hit the hotel pillows until after midnight.

"This is *exhausting*," Lisa said. "I can't believe you do this every week!"

"She finally gets it!" I said to myself. "This is great! Now she knows why I can be so tired when I come home."

One evening the next week, back at home, Lisa was gone — and I was trying to get dinner on the table. Our dog followed me around as if she hadn't been fed in thirty days, even though she had already eaten two meals and two snacks. The kids were all busy with homework: Kelsey asked me how to find the length of a diagonal when the sides of a square are eight inches long, Graham wanted to run some ideas by me about a feature article he needed to do for a writing class, and Allison had to complete a timeline for Israel, Egypt, Greece, and Rome. And I was about to pull out what little hair I have left on the top of my head.

"Was Julius Caesar AD?"

"No, he was BC."

"OK," another kid pushed up to me, "so the sides are eight inches. Now, if I multiply —"

"Just a second, Kelsey, let me just stir this, and I'll look at the problem."

"Dad," Allison cut back in, "when was the fall of Jerusalem?"

"AD 70. You should look it up to be sure, but I'm pretty certain that's right. OK everybody, let's go ahead and eat the salad while the lasagna is settling."

Worse, after I got dinner on the table, the kids still had more homework, so instead of cooking and answering questions, I was now doing dishes and answering questions. And as the clock inched forward, the questions became more desperate: "Daaaad, I think I mixed up the Peloponnesian and the Punic Wars!"

"OK, there were three Punic Wars —"

By the time Lisa walked in the door at 9:30, I was just barely hanging on. Then it dawned on me: While I'm waiting in rental car lines, driving to hotels, and trying to adjust to different time zones, Lisa's at home doing this almost *every night*.

You know what? It's a bear having to travel sometimes. *And* it's a bear trying to cook dinner and help three kids with homework.

Most spouses feel underappreciated. We think our husbands or wives don't understand how difficult we have it, and we're probably right — they usually don't. We're tempted to grow resentful when our hard work is taken for granted. But the truth is, in today's world, *both* spouses usually face a lot of stress. Different stresses, yes, but stress nonetheless. The problem is that, in our narcissism, we assume we have it worse and expect to receive all the empathy, without taking the time to notice the other spouse's challenges. The end result is that both spouses fixate on their own difficulties while remaining blind to the other's challenges, and thus both resent the lack of support they receive from each other.

From a spiritual perspective, this means that pride is the wedge that drives most marriages apart. Looking only to our own situations, we become arrogant, opinionated, and fixated on *our* situations and how our spouses don't appreciate *us*.

Christian marriage invites us to a new way of thinking and acting, a way Paul and the ancients called *humility.* "Each of you should look not only to your own interests," Paul writes, "but also to the interests of others" (Philippians 2:4). This follows an exhortation to consider others "better than yourselves." One commentator suggests how "such a disposition will promote unity, for it binds believers together in mutual interest, respect and appreciation."[33]

Notice this, please: mutual interest, respect, appreciation — all are key virtues for family life, but they're virtues often buried under arrogance, selfishness, and blindness.

Considering our spouses is an *active* charge; it's a decision to spend time actively ruminating on the challenges our spouses must overcome. "But my spouse *doesn't* have it tougher than I do!" some of you are thinking. Notice Paul's next line: "Your attitude should be the same as that of Christ Jesus" (Philippians 2:5).

Look — if Jesus can take this approach, *we* can take this approach!

Pride pushes us away from each other. It exalts itself, it seeks to win arguments, and it aims to advance self and get noticed. Humility draws us toward each other, it seeks to understand, and it aims to achieve intimacy. Pride is one of the greatest enemies of marriage; humility is one of marriage's greatest friends.

Sadly, while pride comes naturally, humility must be pursued. Unless we consciously practice humility in our marriages, we'll naturally fall into a prideful disposition. To help us counteract this, Paul gives us an effective spiritual exercise: Pause for a moment. Don't look only to your own interests — look to the interests of your spouse. Think about him or her. Consider his or her challenges. Empathize with the stress your spouse is feeling. Do this in such a way that you can see how, in some ways, he or she has it tougher than you. Now, show your empathy. Be genuine in your encouragement and support.

Pride is a wedge; humility is a glue. Which spiritual tool will you wield this week?

Worth the Pain

Consider it pure joy, my brothers, whenever you face trials of many kinds, because you know that the testing of your faith develops perseverance. Perseverance must finish its work so that you may be mature and complete, not lacking anything.

James 1:2–4

One of the biggest temptations I face on the road is my attitude toward worship leaders. I'm ashamed to say I have a running feud with these servants of God. While I do my best to fight my negative attitude, it's still difficult for me not to think, as they are being introduced, "So *there's* the enemy."

Whence cometh this sinful disposition?

So many times, a pastor has told me I'll have thirty minutes to preach, but because there's a second service, I need to make sure I quit speaking at, say, 10:10. I then watch as the worship leader goes from chorus to chorus, and then, just in case he thinks we didn't get the message the first thirteen times we sang an earlier song, goes back to it yet one more time for the grand finale. Suddenly my thirty minutes has shrunk to twenty. On the way to the podium I have to mentally cut out a third of my sermon, frantically trying to manufacture new transitions to cover over the points that now will never get delivered.

Recently, I was told I'd have about thirty-five minutes because, the pastor said, "I told the worship leader I want you to have all the time you need." As the service wore on, I looked at my watch — already past the point where I was supposed to be up there — and thought, "Well, I can drop the opening; that's just humor, and it's not really that relevant to the point." As the music kept going, I decided I could drop the point about how this truth related to marriage. Another song dragged on, and I thought, "Well, I can also drop the point about how this applies to parenting, and just make it about our relationship with God." Yet another round, and I thought, "I'll have to drop the second passage from Matthew — I hope the PowerPoint guy can make the jump and skip those slides." Unbeknownst to me, the pastor had been trying to signal "cut" to the worship leader, but she felt so "inspired" she never saw it. When I got behind the pulpit, I looked at the clock and realized I had just fourteen minutes before I was supposed to stop.

That day the church got a sermon summary.

Afterward, I could actually laugh about it with the pastor. God seems determined to make me confront my bitterness over this, and until I do, I fully suspect he's going to "inspire" many other worship leaders to commandeer the service and keep my guest sermons short. Some people may chuckle when I call this a temptation, but it is. My attitude is wrong, and it needs to change. That's a painful and soul-wrenching process.

It's easy to romanticize spiritual growth. It sounds so clean and fulfilling — but the process can actually feel exhausting, frustrating, and very painful. To grow in grace, I have to face ugly realities that truly irritate and inconvenience me — like tyrannical worship leaders! But not just *once*; it seems God is determined to make me face the same situation again and again and again, until his work in my heart gets perfected.

Put in the context of marriage, spiritual growth can even be excruciating. I returned home after that same trip where I had delivered my fourteen-minute sermon summary, and my wife and I faced an issue we've discussed three dozen times if we've discussed it once — but still no progress. Once the issue came up, I became depressed, discouraged, and even more exhausted. Especially coming home from a long trip where God had worked on my attitude toward worship leaders, I wanted to return to a refuge, not a battlefield — but here I was regardless.

It took me two days to break through my funk. Even though the issue never got resolved, I could move past it, following a generous move by Lisa.

But it took two days.

I reveal this because I don't want to imply that the principles put forward in my book *Sacred Marriage* or in *Devotions for a Sacred Marriage* are easy to apply. My wife and I struggle as much as, if not more than, any other couple in living out the truth that is greater than us. Our sinful failings make us just as miserable as they make anyone else. We become just as frustrated, just as exhausted, and just as tired. We think, "Can't we *ever* move past this?"

But these tired moments are the seedbed of growth. I don't like them, but I need them — and so do you. If there were another way, I'm sure God would let us walk it, but there must not be. You will grow so familiar with certain struggles in your marriage that the bad spiritual taste they leave behind can be brought up by memory! It'll help you to remember that such problems aren't a problem just between you and your spouse; they represent the problems of marriage in general. Some issues aren't easily resolved, and some desires may never be fulfilled for the simple reason that *even the best marriage cannot erase the effects of humanity's fall into sin*. It is asking too much to live with another sinful human being without experiencing any tension, any frustration, and any reason to ever practice forgiveness.

It's normal to go through difficult seasons and to occasionally fall into a funk. These are the gritty realities of real marriage. Don't kid yourself. Spiritual growth is not easy; it is about the most difficult exercise known to humankind. But please, don't give up! Seasons of struggle are not the time to evaluate your marriage; they are the time to evaluate *yourself*. The perseverance these seasons produce is worth it.

The catchphrase that helps me press on is this: "I don't like this, but I need it." Repeated often enough, I can even make myself believe it. And sometimes, I can even thank God for its truth — though more often in retrospect than in the moment itself.

Marriage can be difficult; spiritual growth can be exhausting — but they are worth the pain. In the end they produce a far deeper life and a much richer existence than living in a world of superficiality and throwaway relationships.

What Do You Do?

Enjoy life with your wife, whom you love.... For this is your lot in life.

Ecclesiastes 9:9

The hero of *Oblomov*, a Russian novel by Ivan Goncharov, gets asked, "What do you do in life?"

Is there a question we get asked more frequently? Probably not in today's society. Yet this character responds with something refreshingly different: "What? What do I do? Why, I am in love with Olga!"[34]

What a refreshing change of pace for us Westerners! So often, we reply to such a question with a word about our vocations or our hobbies: "I'm an executive at Bank One, and I like to golf and sail on the weekends," or, "I work in marketing for a printing company, and I lead the women's ministry at my church," or even, "I homeschool our three children."

But what, really, is our *biggest* charge? If we're married, isn't loving our spouses at least in the top three? And yet, how often do we mention it or even *think* it? Have you *ever* listed your duty to love your spouse when someone asks you what you do? "What do I do? I focus on loving Bill!" "What do I do? I romance my wife, Melissa."

Maybe it's not helpful to pit vocation against marriage — after all, we do have to earn a living — but isn't something wrong with our sense of priorities, or even our way of thinking, when someone asks us what we do, and loving our spouses doesn't even come to mind?

This may be the core disease of marriage in the West. We don't give enough to it, and we don't derive enough from it. During the week, we're married *after* we work all day, read the newspaper after supper, and watch television all evening. On the weekends, we're married *after* we take the kids to their sporting events; repair what needs fixing; go to church on Sunday; and catch up on laundry, lawn work, and washing the car.

Marriage gets the leftovers — leftover energy, leftover excitement, leftover creativity, and leftover thoughtfulness. We do everything else first, and then, if there's time and we're not exhausted, *then* we'll see if there's something special or loving we can do for our spouses.

I wonder what would happen if we flipped this around, if we started working after we focused on being married; if we fit our play and recreation around our duty to our spouses; if the kids had to occasionally give up something in order for Mom and Dad to get together — instead of the other way around. What would our marriages be like then?

I like Oblomov's response to the question "What do you do in life?"

"What do I do? Why, I am in love with Olga!"

46

Open Marriage

I have chosen the way of truth.

Psalm 119:30

"Gary, do you have anything you want to tell me about?"

"No."

"Nothing about where you went between getting your haircut and picking up Allison at the bus stop?"

"No, not that I can think of."

"I found the evidence. Graham [our son] saw it in your car."

"You know," I said, rising to my own defense, "some wives expect to find other women's phone numbers, or maybe magazines lying around. But an empty Starbucks cup?"

Lisa laughed, but in truth, I do spend more money than I should at Starbucks. We had just bought our own espresso machine, hoping to cut down on the expense, but I was out and about on a winter day, had an extra ten minutes, and could taste the relief even before I bought it. This episode provided just another reminder that everything I do, I do in front of my spouse.

To have or build secrets is to reject the spirit of marriage. The call to become one, the journey toward intimacy, requires an open marriage of honesty and truth. I talked with a man once whose wife suspected he was viewing pornography. He denied it but admitted to keeping a post office box he had never told his wife about. "I can't think of a single good reason to have a secret post office box," I confessed, "but I can think of several bad ones."

The post office box amounted to a giant sinkhole sucking the intimacy out of his marriage. Not surprisingly, he and his wife got divorced several months later. When you start to build a separate life, you pave the way to the ultimate separation — divorce.

Lisa and I laughed one time as we listened to a talk radio host speak with a woman who felt terrible because her husband had caught her going through his wallet. "What's so bad about that?" Lisa wanted to know. Lisa considers my wallet her personal ATM machine. She likes it because it doesn't require a PIN.

Much to our surprise, the host called the woman's actions despicable. The caller fell completely in line, admitting her husband was appalled, confessing she felt ashamed of herself. She proceeded to ask how they could ever get over this "sordid mistake."

Maybe Lisa and I are just weird, but she can go through my wallet anytime she wants to. She knows my email passwords, and I know hers. She has a key for our business post office box. I don't have a single relationship she doesn't know about, and she doesn't have any I don't know about.

It all comes down to this: Are we going to be married, or not? Are we going to be 60 percent married, 75 percent married, 90 percent married, or are we committed to living life together 100 percent as a unit?

The irony is that most of us truly desire to be fully known. That's what creates a sense of belonging and intimacy and fulfillment. But then we create static in our marriage by lying, covering up, or carrying on secret activities. In doing so, we sabotage the very fulfillment we seek. We may lie out of shame, regret, embarrassment, or selfishness, but whenever we do, we strangle the intimacy that comes from knowing and being fully known.

Make the courageous choice to be fully married. When you lie to your spouse, you reject the very spiritual benefits marriage provides: the chance to repent, the motivation to change, the opportunity to be spiritually transformed, the exciting journey of loving and being loved. As soon as you lose the spiritual benefits of marriage, the structure of marriage will start to feel like a restriction instead of an intimate relationship, and the marriage will start to die. You'll lose sight of the purpose and feel overwhelmed by the seemingly negative limitations, and before long, you'll want out. In relationships, deception is the threshold that leads to destruction.

How about if this week you decide to create a new beginning in your relationship — a new honesty and openness, a commitment to truly walk in the light and to choose to "walk in the truth" (3 John 3)? If you've been keeping secrets, this will feel like a new marriage, an entirely new journey. God didn't design a relationship as intense as marriage to be fulfilling when it's done halfway. Be *fully* married, *completely* open and honest with each other.

"I have chosen the way of truth."

The True Image of Love

*So God created man in his own image, in the image of God he
created him; male and female he created them.*

Genesis 1:27

"What does she see in him?"

I'd be surprised if you haven't, at least once in your life, asked this
question about a couple you've met. Maybe the genders were reversed:
"What does he see in her?" but it's likely you, too, have asked this —
or, at the very least, thought it.

I believe the answer is hidden in a divine and prophetic reality.
God has made us in such a way that it is natural for us to grow strongly
attached to someone — on occasion, to someone many others may have
passed over.

Why?

Two realities are going on. First, God has a way of revealing himself to us in surprising places — or, in this case, through surprising
people. Anyone who has any history of walking with God can testify
how God often seems to keep quiet during the weekend fasting
retreat, but while you move the clothes from the washer to the dryer,
or while you shampoo your hair in the shower, he speaks. He has
made us in his own image, and he has the ability and the will to reveal
that image to us as he sees fit.

Keep in mind, Jesus was really and truly the Messiah, the glory
of God behind a human veil — but not everyone saw him that way,
did they? Some saw him as a common man from a common town; others saw him as a threat. Still others saw him as a devil. Only a select
few — indeed, the minority to whom God chose to reveal himself —
saw him as God in flesh.

In the same way, God can reveal himself to you through a person who appears to have comparatively little going for him or her —

but somehow, when love enters the mix, you can't imagine how everyone isn't breaking down the door to get at this incredible person who occupies all your thoughts and fills your heart until it seems about to burst. Just as some see God more clearly in a forest than in a cathedral, so some experience God more fully living with an introvert than an extrovert, or vice versa.

But I also think there's a prophetic dimension to this reaction. Though our future glory as immortals remains masked, we are, in Christ, on the way to this incredible unveiling. Something about love lets us see a glimmer of this future unmasking, even when others remain blinded to it. C. S. Lewis captures this in a famous quote:

> It is a serious thing to . . . remember that the dullest and most uninteresting person you talk to may one day be a creature which, if you saw it now, you would be strongly tempted to worship. . . . It is in the light of these overwhelming possibilities, it is with the awe and the circumspection proper to them, that we should conduct all our dealings with one another, all friendships, all loves, all play, all politics. There are no *ordinary* people. You have never talked to a mere mortal. Nations, cultures, arts, civilization — these are mortal, and their life is to ours as the life of a gnat. But it is immortals whom we joke with, work with, marry, snub, and exploit.[35]

I think it's safe to say that when we lose this sense of awe regarding our spouses — we're married to future immortals we might be tempted to worship if they were fully unmasked — it's not because God has stopped speaking or stopped revealing his nature to us through them, but because we have stopped listening to him and have stopped seeing with his eyes. The failure of married love heralds the onset of coldness toward God; it is a rejection of his presence, his insight, and his amazing dedication to love even the ungrateful and the wicked (Luke 6:35).

If our love begins to fail, it certainly isn't God's perspective that has changed — no, it's ours! The same glory remains hidden behind the facade of that nagging wife or that silent husband. Our resentment or hatred or bitterness may keep us from seeing the hidden glory within, but it's still there.

The maintenance of love requires a partnership with God — what you might even describe as an ongoing act of revelation. We learn to look at these persons as sacred beings made in the image of God and through whom God wants to reveal himself to us.

If mere emotions rule our eyes, we can forget about consistency. I know a man who was eagerly pursued by a young woman over two decades ago. She felt thrilled when he returned her affection. They got married, and for a while she felt delighted to be with him — but her heart grew cold and callous, and she divorced him.

Then this divorced man met a new woman. The new woman seemed just as thrilled with this man as his first wife had been twenty years before. They married, and she can't even begin to imagine why this man's first wife would choose to be alone instead of spending her days with him. The same man elicited three successive reactions — delight, disgust, and then delight once again. Is he truly three different men, or is he simply being viewed through three different lenses?

Love has been compared to a rose, an emotion, a policy, an organ (the heart), a season (spring), and even a physical act (sexual intimacy). But perhaps, to be more biblical, we should see love as a pair of bifocals — the lenses through which we see someone as others don't see them or have stopped seeing them. Instead of changing spouses, maybe all we really need to do is clean our lenses and ask God to show us what he showed us before.

Jesus was the Messiah, though some saw him as the devil. I've talked to some who have gone to both lengths in the way they view their partners. At one point, they saw these persons as temporal saviors, the "missing piece" that gave their lives joy and meaning and purpose. Now these spouses have become the devil incarnate, making their lives miserable. In truth, these men or women were neither messiah nor devil, but merely the clouded lens through which God desires to reveal *himself*.

Your spouse may delight you as well as exasperate you; she may frustrate you as well as overwhelm you with her love. In any situation, during any season, through every emotion, and in every stage of life, your quest should remain the same: to recognize the God who is in and behind the man or woman you love.

"What does she see in him?" some might ask. "What does he see in her?"

The Christian's answer is as shocking as it is true: "I see God, that's what I see. I see *God*."

A Call to Listen

This is my Son, whom I love. Listen to him!

Mark 9:7

Marriage is a call to listen.

Even when our spouses misbehave or create difficult situations for us, we're to tune in to God's still, small voice and ask, "What is it you want me to learn from this? How are you stretching me at this time? What are you trying to do in my soul?"

Instead of listening, our impatient souls immediately want to provide commentary. Our natural, arrogant selves are eager to speak, to be heard, and to be understood. We can't wait to express our opinion, state our outrage, or make clear our intentions; yet the Bible warns, "When words are many, sin is not absent" (Proverbs 10:19).

You know what this tells me in a practical sense? The pause button on my tongue's remote control should get much more use than the play button.

In one of the most remarkable sermons I've ever heard, my friend Darell Smith spoke of his battle with multiple sclerosis. He talked about how for years he kept asking God, "Why?" But finally he learned to ask a more appropriate question: "What?" "*What* is it, God, that you want me to learn from this? What lessons do I need to practice? What character issue are you eager to transform?"

"Why" questions are interrogations; we're asking for an explanation. "What" questions humbly ask for insight. "Why" questions assume God has to defend himself; "what" questions more correctly put the onus on *us*: how do *we* need to change?

Marriage is a brilliant school for the art of listening. If you're at all like me, listening will initially feel almost like an unnatural act, requiring supernatural assistance. When I'm angry or feel put out, I don't want to listen to *anyone*, God included; I want to state my case.

But God knew what he was doing when he called us into marriage. Listening is an active discipline, and in our sin we are passive people. Listening requires tremendous motivation and about as much humility as any spiritual obligation we'll ever accept. It also provides the foundation for our spiritual health. Jesus spent a good bit of his time urging people to just listen:

- "Listen and understand" (Matthew 15:10).
- "He who has ears to hear, let him hear" (Mark 4:9).
- "Again Jesus called the crowd to him and said, 'Listen to me, everyone, and understand this'" (Mark 7:14).
- "Consider carefully how you listen" (Luke 8:18).
- "Listen carefully to what I am about to tell you" (Luke 9:44).
- "My sheep listen to my voice" (John 10:27).

Listening is the motor oil for both spiritual growth and marital health. Without it, the friction and the heat will cause the gears of our souls to jam and break, blowing up the engine. Relationships start to break down when both parties keep talking and stop listening. Being together, building intimacy, and growing in oneness *require* listening. When we stop listening, we stop loving.

It all begins with our prayers. If we keep rattling off a list of things we want God to change about our spouses, we're not paying attention to the list of things God wants to use our spouses to change about *us*. My morning prayers have become virtual marching orders. God almost never points out something my wife needs to do for me; ninety-nine times out of a hundred, he reveals to me what I'm to do for her.

Listening, of course, requires a monumental shift in attitude. We should enter each day of marriage as learners, not teachers. God uses the challenges of marriage to teach us about ourselves. He uses our spouses to teach us how the other gender thinks and reacts. He uses marriage to give us perspective, and perhaps even a new outlook. God does not limit his lessons according to the gifting of the persons with whom we live; he is well able to speak through even the worst of sinners.

But when we refuse to listen, we miss all this. You can change the entire spiritual climate in your home merely by choosing to listen. It's amazing what this simple spiritual act can do. Days of despair get transformed into days of discovery; disappointment gives way to discernment.

The best way to change your marriage is to start listening more than you talk. And when you pray, listen to God more than you complain about your spouse. Use your ears, and watch how God uses those floppy appendages to reawaken your heart. I have found that God can use *any* situation in life to teach me something, if only I'll listen for that lesson.

This week, listen — for a change, for a new life, and for a new marriage.

The Estate of Marriage

For this reason a man will leave his father and mother and be united to his wife, and they will become one flesh.

Genesis 2:24

It always amazes me how contemporary ancient works can be. Martin Luther penetrated the twenty-first century when he gazed into the souls of sixteenth-century couples in his essay titled "The Estate of Marriage." Since we live in a day when marriage is coming under increasing attack, we would do well to listen to Luther's words.

Luther begins his essay by reminding us that respect for marriage flows from acknowledging the One who designed marriage — God: "Do not criticize this work, or call that evil which he himself has called good. He knows better than you yourself what is good and to your benefit, as he says in Genesis [2:18], 'it is not good that the man should be alone.'"[36]

Luther urged his listeners to ignore the "pagan" voices decrying marriage:

> Young men should be on their guard when they read pagan books and hear the common complaints about marriage, lest they inhale poison. For the estate of marriage does not set well with the devil, because it is God's good will and work. This is why the devil has contrived to have so much shouted and written in the world against the institution of marriage, to frighten men away from this godly life and entangle them in a web of fornication and secret sins. . . . The world says of marriage, "brief is the joy, lasting the bitterness." Let them say what they please; what God wills and creates is bound to be a laughingstock to them.

In Luther's mind, it is not enough merely to be married; we must appreciate God's purpose in calling us into marriage. God calls us into family life to shape our souls and to create a stable foundation for the next generation:

> To recognize the estate of marriage is something quite different from merely being married. He who is married but does not recognize the estate of marriage cannot continue in wedlock without bitterness, drudgery, and anguish; he will inevitably complain and blaspheme like the pagans and blind, irrational men. . . . Now the ones who recognize the estate of marriage are those who firmly believe that God himself instituted it, brought husband and wife together, and ordained that they should beget children and care for them. For this they have God's word [Genesis 1:28], and they can be certain that he does not lie. They can therefore also be certain that the estate of marriage and everything that goes with it in the way of conduct, works, and suffering is pleasing to God. Now tell me, how can the heart have greater good, joy, and delight than in God, when one is certain that his estate, conduct, and work is pleasing to God?

This assurance that *God has called us into marriage* will most help us when marriage becomes a struggle. Luther urges us to remember that even the most difficult aspects of wedlock can bring joy when we see them as part of God's plan for us. Certain "blind" people run from the challenges of marriage because

> they fail to see that their life and conduct with their wives is the work of God and pleasing in his sight. Could they but find that then no wife would be so hateful, so ill-tempered, so ill-mannered, so poor, so sick that they would fail to find in her their hearts' delight. . . . And because they see that it is the good pleasure of their beloved Lord, they would be able to have peace in grief, joy in the midst of bitterness, happiness in the midst of tribulations, as the martyrs have in suffering.

In Luther's view, because God has created marriage, we, God's children and followers, should embrace *all* aspects of it — even the tough parts — because we know it is his will and his design. But when life's pleasantness becomes more important than the spiritual foundations, we lose the discernment to appreciate marriage:

> We err in that we judge the work of God according to our own feelings, and regard not his will but our own desire. This is why we are unable to recognize his works and persist in making evil that which is good, and regarding as bitter that which is pleasant. Nothing is so bad, not even death itself, but what it becomes sweet and tolerable if only I know and am certain that it is pleasing to God.

Luther sums up the estate of marriage this way:

> I say these things in order that we may learn how honorable a thing it is to live in that estate which God has ordained. In it we find God's word and good pleasure, by which all the works, conduct, and sufferings of that estate become holy, godly, and precious so that Solomon even congratulates such a man and says in Proverbs, "Rejoice in the wife of your youth," and again in Ecclesiastes, "Enjoy life with the wife whom you love all the days of your vain life." Solomon ... is offering godly comfort to those who find much drudgery in married life.

While *Devotions for a Sacred Marriage* isn't a book on the theology of marriage, it's essential for us to possess a basic theological understanding of marriage, and that understanding is this: God designed and created marriage as a lifelong institution between one man and one woman, and he calls most of us into this estate. The fact that he created marriage and called us into marriage makes this estate a holy one, a right one, and a spiritually healthy one. We should humbly surrender to God's will.

Armed with this understanding and insight, even the most difficult of marriages have value. To requote Luther, "Now tell me, how can the heart have greater good, joy, and delight than in God, when one is certain that his estate, conduct, and work is pleasing to God?"

God designed this relationship. God called you into this relationship. Therefore, marriage — with all its joy and all its trials, all its comforts and all its sufferings, all its happiness and all its pain — is good.

Passive Persecution

I opened for my lover,
but my lover had left; he was gone....
I looked for him but did not find him.
I called him but he did not answer.

Song of Songs 5:6

An entire category of wounding in marriage receives little notice, though it wreaks great havoc on many relationships. For lack of a better phrase, I call it *passive persecution*.

There is a moment in a marriage when neglect — a passive reality — becomes persecution — an active wound. What is withheld starts hurting, and it becomes a living irritant. Its devastation grows worse when the sore wound gets regularly pummeled by continued neglect.

What makes passive persecution so pernicious is that those who cause the injury almost never realize it, or if they do, they minimize the pain their partners feel. "I'm not doing anything," they protest — but that's precisely the point! It's their "not doing anything" that hurts so much.

When a man can go an entire week without having a single conversation with his wife that goes beyond utilitarian purposes; when he can go two weeks without inquiring about how his wife is really feeling, what went on inside her when her sister accused her of something or a friend stood her up — she suffers an ongoing wound. The first cut came when she recognized the neglect, thinking, "He let me down." The second cut comes when her husband doesn't even realize their emotional intimacy has dipped to about 1.5 on a scale of 1 to 10.

It's only a matter of time until "He let me down" becomes "He doesn't even care that he let me down." Now it's no longer an event that upset her; it's turned into an ongoing assault. It won't be long before disappointment morphs into resentment, resentment evolves into bitterness, and then, more often than not, the husband will eventually run into an explosion of bottled-up emotions suddenly unleashed over the seemingly smallest event: "So I forgot you had a doctor's appointment today and didn't ask you about it; what's the big deal? Does that make me a bad husband?"

Men often feel passive persecution in the bedroom. When a man gets denied, regularly put off, or even just not approached, after a season he starts to hurt, as if something active were being done to him. Every day feels like a wound. The wife may think, "We had sex a week ago; we've been busy. What's the big deal?" But he's thinking, "It's now been seven days," and the silence of the last five nights feels like a slap in the face — yet another malicious assault. The wife thinks nothing is being done, but that *nothing* feels like *something* to her husband. And he begins to shut down.

I don't know how else to describe it, but something takes place in a sexually neglected man's soul. He doesn't just step back physically; he removes part of himself spiritually and emotionally as well. In spiritually acute situations, he may begin to look elsewhere, even if only through his eyes or in his thoughts, which can open the door to any number of evils our fallen world eagerly exploits.

Passive persecution doesn't have a unilateral remedy. Many times, it's born in high expectations, and the spouse who feels persecuted will need to reevaluate his or her disappointment and honestly explore whether the offense he or she is feeling springs more from narcissistic self-focus and demands than from true, honest neglect.

But this is not to say that the offended spouse may not have a case — in most instances, they *do*. Marriage asks so much of us that it's inevitable we will let things slip. When we do, it's our responsibility to ask for forgiveness, sincerely try to empathize with our spouses' feelings of abandonment and hurt, and pledge ourselves to get better at providing active care.

Here's a word picture that may help: let's say you're on a hike with your spouse. It's hot, and you feel like you'd kill for a drink of water. You're so thirsty your body has started to shut down, so that almost all you can think about is something to drink. Your spouse keeps staying just far enough ahead of you that when you cry out, he can't hear your voice. He finally stops at a lookout, allowing you to catch up, and you watch as he consumes the last swallow of Gatorade.

"Give me some of that!" you say, only to hear, "Sorry, that was the last drop; didn't *you* bring any?"

"I'm out, and I'm dying of thirst!"

"Oh well, there's a stream a few more miles up the trail; it shouldn't take us more than another hour or so."

You'd probably be furious at your spouse, and understandably so. In that wilderness, he represented your only source of refreshment. It may not have been his fault that you're so thirsty, but certainly, he could have eased your pain and yet chose not to or, at least, simply neglected to consider you.

What aren't you hearing today? What neglect, what passive persecution, might you be leveling against your spouse at this very moment? There are some things in life *only* a spouse can provide; if you deny these things, it becomes an absolute denial.

Here's a challenge: why not ask your spouse, "Hey, are you thirsty? If so, in what way?" I've talked to enough couples to know there's almost always at least one area in which your spouse feels neglected. The duties of marriage are too many and too diverse for that not to be the case.

Let's allow kindness and even generosity to govern us. The person you're talking to took a tremendous risk. Out of all the billions of people on the face of the earth, he or she chose to spend this life with *you*. When your spouse made this decision, he or she put himself or herself at your mercy, since, as we said before, there are certain things only a spouse can provide. Let's honor that trust with open hands and enthusiastic hearts. You may think you're not doing anything, but remember that "not doing anything" can well be a direct assault on your spouse: "You gave no water to the weary and you withheld food from the hungry" (Job 22:7).

Is that how you want to be remembered? By what you *didn't* do?

Kindness Matters

Love is kind.

1 Corinthians 13:4

"What five or six qualities would you choose in a mate if you were looking for a wife?" someone once asked me.

After some thought, I rattled off six items.

"You didn't even mention physical appearance," said the man.

"Hmmm," I said. But after thinking about it some more, I realized the omission was no accident.

"Let's say you were married to Charlize Theron," I explained. "For the sake of argument, let's say you've been married for seven years. If you're rushing to get ready for work and she comes out of the shower stark naked, you know what you're going to say? 'Honey, have you seen my brown belt? I can't find my belt and I need to leave in ten minutes.' As crazy as it may sound, you would actually be more excited at the sight of that leather belt than you would be watching your naked wife walk to the closet."

The way we're wired, physical attraction of even the highest nature, over time, quiets down. Sometimes I forget I'm married to a very attractive woman. I see her every day, and so it's easy to take it for granted. But you know what I *don't* take for granted? Every individual act of kindness.

For some reason, I never seem to grow callous toward kindness. In fact, just this morning, as I was trying to get back into my office, my wife saw I was preparing a cup of chai and said, "Here, let me get that for you."

"You sure?"

"Yeah. Go down to your office; I'll bring it to you."

I'm sipping the tea as I write this, getting my midmorning caffeine boost and thinking very pleasant thoughts about my wife.

I say in *Sacred Marriage* that most couples don't fall out of love; they fall out of repentance.[37] It's our selfish, unkind attitudes that poison our affection for each other far more than anything else, and it's our acts of generosity and kindness that keep intimacy alive.

I was speaking spiritually, but now, apparently, there's sociological evidence to back this up. Dr. John Gottman is a professor of psychology at the University of Washington and one of today's foremost authorities on what makes marriages work and what leads to divorce. Listen to his words:

> At the heart of my program is the simple truth that happy marriages are based on a deep friendship. By this I mean a mutual respect for and enjoyment of each other's company. These couples tend to know each other intimately — they are well versed in each other's likes, dislikes, personality quirks, hopes, and dreams. They have an abiding regard for each other and express this fondness not just in the big ways but in little ways day in and day out.[38]

These "little ways" are nothing more than practical expressions of kindness. Listen to how this worked its way out in a couple known by Dr. Gottman:

> Take the case of hardworking Nathaniel, who runs his own import business and works very long hours. In another marriage, his schedule might be a major liability. But he and his wife, Olivia, have found ways to stay connected. They talk frequently on the phone during the day. When she has a doctor's appointment, he remembers to call to see how it went. When he has a meeting with an important client, she'll check in to see how it fared. When they have chicken for dinner, she gives him both drumsticks because she knows he likes them best. When he makes blueberry pancakes for the kids on Saturday morning, he'll leave the blueberries out of hers because he knows she doesn't like them. Although he's not religious, he accompanies her to church each Sunday because it's important to her. And although she's not crazy about spending a lot of time with their relatives, she has pursued a friendship with Nathaniel's mother and sisters because family matters so much to him.[39]

Romantic feelings come and go, but biblical love is supported by *chosen* thoughtfulness and kindness. Nathaniel doesn't want to go to church, but he goes because it's important to his wife. Olivia doesn't particularly enjoy having a close relationship with her husband's family, but she wants to please her husband, so she makes the effort. In other words, they *choose* to be kind, and that kindness colors their entire relationship.

Dr. Gottman suggests that consistent, small acts of kindness provide a surer foundation than sporadic romantic vacations and extravagant anniversary gifts. Paul gave this same prescription two thousand years ago in much fewer words when he wrote, "Love is kind." We can choose to transform the climate in our homes by adopting these attitudes of godliness — patience, gentleness, selflessness, kindness, love — which the Bible urges us to adopt. Conversely, the things Paul says love is *not* are the very qualities that make home life so miserable: "It does not envy, it does not boast, it is not proud. It is not rude, it is not self-seeking, it is not easily angered, it keeps no record of wrongs" (1 Corinthians 13:4–5).

In other words, a satisfying marital experience has far more to do with character than emotional attraction, romantic feelings, sexual acumen, or physical appeal. As believers filled with God's Holy Spirit, we can choose to be kind. We can choose to be patient. We can choose to be gentle. But when virtue becomes a stranger, any relationship will begin to sour.

I stand by what I wrote several years ago: Most couples don't fall out of love; they fall out of repentance.

52

Oases of Sanity

*He is like a tree planted by streams of water,
which yields its fruit in season
and whose leaf does not wither.*

Psalm 1:3

Thanks to the hospitality of the Hawthorne Gospel Church in Newark, New Jersey, Lisa and I got to spend two days in New York City without the kids. Since we had already visited the city with our children, we were able to do more "grown-up" things. Lisa wanted to find some "funky shops"; we thought we should take in a Broadway or off-Broadway play and eat at some exotic ethnic restaurants.

Even though I've been to New York several times, it's hard to get used to Times Square, particularly at night. There's a desperate grab for your attention, and the tacky commercialism hits you from all directions. At night, eighty-foot video advertisements shine on buildings, gigantic billboards light up, and 3-D sculptures hawk the latest cell phones and cars. Then there are the eccentric people, such as the colorfully dressed religious groups passing out literature, or the "Naked Cowboy" — a guy who wears barely legal briefs, covered by his guitar, and charges you to have your picture taken with him (we politely declined).

We attended two plays, one of which at the time was considered to be the best and biggest play on Broadway. Everybody we talked to said, "If you're going to see only one play, you need to see this one." We saw it — and we felt shocked at its raunchiness. As people filed out of the theater, raving over the performance, we thought we were living in a world where everything had been turned upside down. "Are we really *that* out of touch?" we asked each other.

But then, on our way to Central Park, we passed David Wilkerson's Times Square Church. Something almost monumental happened in my soul at the sight of that otherwise nondescript building. I took a huge spiritual breath, as though I'd been holding it for days and only now had permission to let it out. This relatively simple church provided a physical reminder of a different life, a different purpose, a deeper calling — a quiet oasis in a noisy city. We didn't go in (it was a Saturday), but it was uplifting just to be reminded of the reality this church represents.

It struck me that, spiritually, we live in the middle of Times Square. Movies, books, music, advertisements, magazines (even if you don't read them, you see the covers in the grocery stores), and television all carry various messages about sex, marriage, dating, and family life. It's like a daily assault on our spiritual senses. If we don't seek out oases of sanity, we can become buried by the world's conflicting messages.

I pray that *Devotions for a Sacred Marriage* has been one of those oases for you — because we need many. If we don't consciously remind ourselves of the spiritual purpose of marriage, the Christian's duty to be God-centered in marriage, the greater good of marriage, and God's design for marriage, we'll soon get buried by the world's caricatures, advertisements, and lies. We'll begin asking of our marriage what God didn't design it to give, while discounting those aspects of marriage that God does intend but that the world doesn't value.

Though you've reached the end of this year of devotions, I hope it's just one vacation among many you'll take in the future. I hope you continue to find materials that inspire you to remain devoted to each other as an expression of your love for God.

I hope you'll also influence others, reminding them of the goodness of marriage as God designed it — the way that holiness serves a family better than any illicit excitement ever invented by the devil; the way that a proper spiritual perspective can turn even the trials of marriage into sweet opportunities for growth. For not only do we need the Times Square churches to point us back to real life; we can become Times Square churches in our own communities. Each godly marriage can be an oasis for those who have forgotten what marriage is supposed to look like.

With great challenges come great rewards; that's what I'd tell a couple contemplating marriage. You're about to be challenged as you've never been challenged before, but the struggle is worth it. The pain is worth it. Because through it all, you'll experience life as God created it and called you to live it, and there is absolutely no better place to be in this world than the place God has ordained for you.

Notes

1. Cited in Cal Fussman, "Al Pacino," *Esquire* (July 2002), 110–12.
2. Terri Orbuch et al., "Marital Quality Over the Life Course," *Social Psychology Quarterly* 59 (June 1996), 162–72.
3. I discuss this more fully in my book *Authentic Faith* (Grand Rapids: Zondervan, 2002), 235–41.
4. Cited in Rick Reilly, "A Paragon Rising above the Madness," *Sports Illustrated* (March 20, 2000), 136.
5. Cited in Carolyn Mahaney, *Feminine Appeal* (Wheaton, Ill.: Crossway, 2003), 7.
6. C. J. Mahaney, *Sex, Romance, and the Glory of God: What Every Husband Needs to Know* (Wheaton, Ill.: Crossway, 2004), 56–57.
7. Cited in *The Little Flowers of St. Francis*, trans. Raphael Brown (New York: Doubleday, 1958), 92–93.
8. J. W. L. Hoad, "Mercy, Merciful," in *The New Bible Dictionary*, ed. J. D. Douglas (Grand Rapids: Eerdmans, 1962), 809.
9. Cited in Mahaney, *Sex, Romance, and the Glory of God*, 42.
10. Reported in Barbara Dafoe Whitehead and David Popenoe, "Who Wants to Find a Soul Mate" (National Marriage Project, June 2001); can be viewed on the Web at http://marriage.rutgers.edu/Publications/SOOU/TEXTSOOU2001.htm.
11. Clement of Alexandria, cited in John E. L. Oulton and Henry Chadwick, eds., *Alexandrian Christianity: Selected Translations of Clement and Origen* (Philadelphia: Westminster, 1954), 71.
12. Andrew Murray, *Humility*, rev. ed. (Springdale, Pa.: Whitaker House, 1982), 44.
13. Elton and Pauline Trueblood, *The Recovery of Family Life* (New York: Harper & Row, 1953), 56–57.
14. Cited in Dana Mack and David Blankenhorn, eds., *The Book of Marriage* (Grand Rapids: Eerdmans, 2001), 467.
15. Story and quotes taken from Rick Reilly, *Who's Your Caddy?* (New York: Doubleday, 2003), 246 and following.
16. Reilly, *Who's Your Caddy?* 255.
17. Gene Stratton-Porter, *Freckles* (Wheaton, Ill.: Tyndale House, 2000), 1. Note: The actual text is written in accent. I Anglicized it to make it easier to read.
18. Ibid., 17.
19. Paul Evdokimov, *The Sacrament of Love* (Crestwood, N.Y.: St. Vladimir's Seminary Press, 1985), 112.

20. Cited in Mack and Blankenhorn, *The Book of Marriage*, 199.
21. Henry Drummond, *The Greatest Thing in the World* (London: Collins, 1930), 51.
22. Ibid., 57.
23. Ibid.
24. Ibid., 57–58.
25. Ibid., 52.
26. Ibid.
27. Ibid., 54.
28. I cover in greater detail the virtue of detachment in my book *The Glorious Pursuit: Embracing the Virtues of Christ* (Colorado Springs: NavPress, 1998).
29. Pat Conroy, *My Losing Season* (New York: Doubleday, 2002), 143.
30. C. F. Keil, *The First Book of Moses* (Grand Rapids: Eerdmans, 1949), 103.
31. Nancy Belcher, "Venice Marathon: An American Runner in Venice," *Northwest Runner* (February 2004), 27.
32. This quote and the others used in this devotion are taken from an essay compiled by Joseph Kerns, "The Theology of Marriage," in Mack and Blankenhorn, *The Book of Marriage*, 405 and following.
33. Jac Muller, *The Epistles of Paul to the Philippians and to Philemon*, New International Commentary on the New Testament (Grand Rapids: Eerdmans, rep. 1980), 75.
34. Ivan Goncharov, *Oblomov* (New York: Macmillan, 1915).
35. C. S. Lewis, *The Weight of Glory* (Grand Rapids: Eerdmans, 1949), 14–15.
36. This quote and others in this devotion are from Mack and Blankenhorn, *The Book of Marriage*, 368.
37. See Gary Thomas, *Sacred Marriage* (Grand Rapids: Zondervan, 2000), 96.
38. Cited in Mack and Blankenhorn, *The Book of Marriage*, 466.
39. Ibid., 467.

Acknowledgments

As always with a book of this sort, I need to first thank my wife, Lisa, not only for walking this life with me, but also for being so gracious to open up our lives for the benefit of others and for being so instrumental in the editing process. Several friends reviewed these devotions and made many helpful suggestions, including Todd and Lisa Fetters, Annie Carlson, Brad and Mary Kay Smith, Byron Weathersbee, and Dave and Dina Horne. Thanks are due to Dirk Buursma for his customary good care of the manuscript during the editing process, as well as to the baristas at the Barkley Village Starbucks. Thanks for keeping the chai teas (seven pumps, nonfat, extra hot) coming! I also owe a big debt to John Sloan at Zondervan. One day I merely mentioned the idea of a marriage devotional book and, much to my surprise, discovered a contract offer in the mail a few months later — no agent; no haggling, no hassle, not even a proposal. This has been, without a doubt, the easiest publishing process I've ever been through!

Gary Thomas

Please feel free to contact Gary. Although he can't respond personally to all correspondence, he'd love to receive your feedback:

Gary Thomas
P.O. Box 29417
Bellingham, WA 98228-1417
email: GLT3@aol.com

For information about Gary's ministry and his speaking schedule, visit his website at www.garythomas.com. To inquire about inviting Gary to your church, please write or call the Center for Evangelical Spirituality at 360-676-7773, or email Laura at Laura@garythomas.com.

The Center for Evangelical Spirituality (CFES) is a ministry dedicated to fostering spiritual growth within the Christian community through an integrated study of Scripture, church history, and the Christian classics. We believe evangelical Christians can learn a great deal from historic Christian traditions without compromising the essential tenets of what it means to be an evangelical Christian. Accepting Scripture as our final and absolute authority, we seek to promote Christian growth and the refinement of an authentic Christian spirituality.

What If God Designed Marriage to Make Us Holy More Than to Make Us Happy?

Sacred Marriage

Gary Thomas

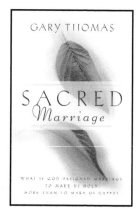

Your marriage is more than a sacred covenant with another person. It is a spiritual discipline designed to help you know God better, trust him more fully, and love him more deeply.

Scores of books have been written that offer guidance for building the marriage of your dreams. But what if God's primary intent for your marriage isn't to make you happy . . . but holy? And what if your relationship isn't as much about you and your spouse as it is about you and God?

This book may very well alter profoundly the contours of your marriage. It will most certainly change you. Because whether it is delightful or difficult, your marriage can become a doorway to a closer walk with God, and to a spiritual integrity that, like salt, seasons the world around you with the savor of Christ.

Softcover: 0-310-24282-7

Pick up a copy today at your favorite bookstore!

ZONDERVAN™

GRAND RAPIDS, MICHIGAN 49530 USA

WWW.ZONDERVAN.COM

Sacred Parenting

Gary L. Thomas

Many books have been written about how to parent a child effectively, how to become a better parent, and how effective parenting produces better kids. But *Sacred Parenting* delves into a different reality: how parenting affects the parent. It explores the spiritual dynamics of parenting, and why caring for children is such an effective discipline in shaping our souls and forming the character of Christ within us. Parents of all children will be encouraged by seeing how others have successfully handled the challenges of parenting and will be inspired by stories that reaffirm the spiritual value of being a parent.

Softcover: 0-310-26451-0

Devotions for Sacred Parenting

A Year of Weekly Devotions for Parents

Gary L. Thomas

Spend time once a week for an entire year contemplating the soul-transforming journey of parenting.

Devotions for Sacred Parenting continues this journey with fifty-two short devotions, containing all new material. The life-related devotions are creative and fresh, and readers will be inspired, challenged, and encouraged as they explore the spiritual joys and challenges of raising children. Each devotion will point them to opportunities for spiritual growth—and help them become more effective parents at the same time.

Hardcover: 0-310-25596-1

We want to hear from you. Please send your comments about this book to us in care of zreview@zondervan.com. Thank you.

ZONDERVAN™

GRAND RAPIDS, MICHIGAN 49530 USA

WWW.ZONDERVAN.COM